Los Angeles—

Struggles toward

Multiethnic Community

Asian American,

African American,

& Latino Perspectives

Los Angeles— Struggles toward Multiethnic Community

Asian American, African American, & Latino Perspectives

Edited by
Edward T. Chang
& Russell C. Leong

University of Washington Press
Seattle and London

Library of Congress Cataloging-in-Publication Data
Los Angeles—struggles toward multiethnic community : Asian American, African
American, and Latino perspectives / edited by Edward T. Chang and Russell C. Leong.
— 1st University of Washington Press ed.
    p. cm.
    "Originally published in 1993 by the Asian American Studies Center, UCLA,
as volume 19, no. 2 of Amerasia journal"—T.p. verso.
ISBN 0-295-97375-7 (alk. paper)
    1. Los Angeles (Calif.)—Ethnic relations. I. Chang, Edward T. II. Leong, Russell C.
F869.L89A24   1994   94-32758
305.8'00979493—dc20   CIP

The paper used in this publication meets the minimum requirements of American
National Standard for Information Sciences—Permanence of Paper for Printed Library
Materials, ANSI Z39.48-1984.

Cover photograph by Eugene Ahn: At Western and 15th in Los Angeles, schoolchildren pass
the mural of Madame Shin-sa-im-dang (1504-51), a poet and painter of the Yi Dynasty
who in Korea today symbolizes the talented, beautiful, accomplished woman and
virtuous wife and mother.

Contents

Commentary

Preface
The Making of "Los Angeles—Struggles toward Multiethnic Community"

RUSSELL C. LEONG

In the City of Angels, the fire and smoke had not yet begun. Three years prior to the L.A. uprising, Edward Chang and I were grabbing a quick meal in a fast food restaurant in the heart of Koreatown in Los Angeles. The family-run Korean eatery was located in a brand-new indoor mall near Western and Olympic avenues. Inside the mall we could see Koreans, but—with the exception of one strolling couple—African Americans were noticeably absent. If one looked carefully, Latino men were present, usually lifting, cutting, or bagging in the supermarket or tucked behind counters in the restaurant kitchens. Partly because of their height and dark hair, which are similar in Asians, the Latinos did not stand out. Yet, we could not take their "blending" for granted; indeed, growing numbers of Asians and Latinos especially in Los Angeles were changing the complexion of race relations, which could no longer be defined as Black and White.

As we ate our noodles and *kim chee*, Edward and I talked about the 1990 Red Apple Grocery boycott in Brooklyn, New York, and about the economic conflicts and racial tensions that were bound to escalate in South Central Los Angeles. Previously all-Black neighborhoods were now predominately Latino; Korean-owned stores had replaced Jewish-owned ones in the same communities. Edward, a Korean American sociologist

RUSSELL C. LEONG is the editor of *Amerasia Journal*, published by the UCLA Asian American Studies Center.

and civil rights activist, and myself, a Chinese American poet and editor, from our different vantage points, could see the racial clock ticking. The broad face of the clock was white, but the moving hands, numbers, and hours were black. But where did the Asians and Latinos fit in this timely scheme of things?

We concluded that one key to building multiethnic community was through education—teaching our own communities about one another: Asian, Latino, African American. We knew we had a vehicle for education in the *Amerasia Journal*, the national interdisciplinary publication of UCLA's Asian American Studies Center, with its editorial board and dedicated staff. We began to contact individuals who we knew were committed to analyzing race and ethnic relations in this city and in the nation and who were not afraid to tackle their controversial and contradictory aspects. But the Rodney King case, the Latasha Harlins killing, and the L.A. uprising occurred as we were putting together a special issue of the journal, and the articles had to be constantly revised during the editing process. Ella Stewart completed her study of communication patterns between Korean and African Americans before the uprising, for example, and then spent many months revising it to reflect conditions after the crisis.

The present volume, based upon this 1993 special issue of *Amerasia Journal*, focuses on race and ethnic relations in Los Angeles as they have emerged from the uprising and as they exist in the broader national picture. The uprising revealed that radical approaches are needed to address structured social, economic, and political inequality and pressing issues of race and representation in the literature, media, and culture.

Our goal for this volume was to gather a variety of academic and journalistic perspectives and commentary, as well as creative and literary approaches to building multiethnic community. Scholarly essays include "Jewish and Korean Merchants in African American Neighborhoods," by Edward Chang; "Communication between African Americans and Korean Americans: Before and After the Los Angeles Riots," by Ella Stewart; "Asian Americans and Latinos in San Gabriel Valley, California," by Leland Saito; "The South Central Los Angeles Eruption: A Latino Perspective," by Armando Navarro; "Race, Class, Conflict and Empowerment: On Ice Cube's Black Korea," by Jeff Chang, and "Which Side Are You On?" by Arvli Ward. Commentaries by Asian and African American writers feature Larry Aubry, Angela E. Oh, Sharon Park, Amy Uyematsu, Erich Nakano, Walter Lew, and Miriam Ching Louie.

A special feature of this collection is a section entitled "Seoul to Soul" that showcases literary writings by African and Asian American writers and artists from Los Angeles, including Mari Sunaida, Ko Won, Wanda

Coleman, Mellonee Houston, Sae Lee, Nat Jones, Arjuna, Chungmi Kim, and Lynn Manning. "Seoul to Soul" was based on the first reading by Black and Korean writers held in Los Angeles, which took place before the L.A. uprising.

Los Angeles has emerged as a focal point for social scientists as they develop new ideas about race relations, questioning previous theories and notions of the American melting pot and of a pluralistic society. We hope that *Los Angeles—Struggles toward Multiethnic Community* opens and stimulates the dialogue among groups that previously were speaking in limited ways with one another, and that it will encourage us to examine our own communities, wherever we may live in the United States, in fresh, critical, and constructive ways.

Acknowledgments

We would like to acknowledge each author's vital contribution that made this multiethnic collection possible: Ella Stewart, Leland Saito, Armando Navarro, Jeff Chang, Arvli Ward, Mari Sunaida, Ko Won, Wanda Coleman, Mellonee R. Houston, Sae Lee, Nat Jones, Arjuna, Chungmi Kim, Lynn Manning, Larry Aubry, Angela E. Oh, Sharon Park, Amy Uyematsu, Erich Nakano, Walter Lew, and Miriam Ching Yoon Louie. We thank the UCLA Asian American Studies Center and its director, Don T. Nakanishi, for their support. *Amerasia Journal* staff members who contributed to the editing and proofreading of the journal included Glenn Omatsu, labor activist and associate editor of *Amerasia Journal*; Mary Kao, production and design; and Jean Pang Yip, business manager and proofreader. Eugene Ahn provided the cover image and photographs for the issue.

Los Angeles—
Struggles toward Multiethnic Community

Introduction
From Chicago to Los Angeles—Changing the Site of Race Relations

Edward T. Chang

As smoke darkened the skies of Los Angeles, the issue of race took center stage. The city's civil unrest of 1992 brought forth new thinking and new questions about race relations in America. Myths and theories of the melting pot, of assimilation and of the plural society were shattered as racial violence vividly exposed the inadequacy of our prior assumptions. What is race? What is ethnicity? What does it mean to live in a multiethnic society? Can we truly live together in such a society?

The Kerner Commission Report of 1968 had concluded that America was headed toward two societies—one black and the other white—separate but unequal. Twenty-five years later, we must conclude that the commission report was only partially correct in its projections. Los Angeles' civil unrest was America's first multiethnic "riot" as Latino immigrants, Korean merchants, African American residents and Whites participated as both victims and assailants. As we begin to sort things out to understand exactly what happened, many pressing questions remain. One of the most troubling questions, in my view, is: Why do we lack the theories to explain what happened?

The lack of theoretical models leads us to evaluate the relevancy of traditional social science research in looking at society. Critics of mainstream academia have asserted that race relations research in the United States has had little connection to social reality. Sociology had become a science of methodology devoted to the proving of theories. The prevalance of positivist scholarship simplified sociology to the level of data collection and survey. Moreover, social scientists were themselves disengaged from social reality in their insistence on interpreting events

EDWARD T. CHANG is an assistant professor of ethnic studies at the University of California, Riverside.

from an "objective" perspective. Scholars and researchers were far more interested in constructing theories and in validating them than in understanding the "hows" and the "whys" of social change or of cultural and political upheaval.

For example, whenever I have presented findings about the roles of Korean immigrants in small business, sociologists ask me: "But what are the theoretical implications of your research?" It appears that we have forgotten that, bottom line, theory is only theory. Theory may be a useful tool in providing explanations of social phenomena, but social science also needs to provide adequate interpretations of social reality for the people and the communities that it is studying.

Studies have shown that economic inequality and pervasive poverty in urban America contributed to the civil unrest of the 1960s. The unrest of 1992 was no different. What are the causes of racial and ethnic inequality in America? Why are certain groups able to move out of ethnic ghettos while other groups remain? How can underprivileged groups uplift themselves and enter the mainstream? These were, and continue to be, among the major questions that social scientists address in race relations research.

*   *   *

During the early twentieth century, Chicago had become the site of race and ethnic research as millions of Jews, Poles, Blacks, and Irish settled in that midwestern city. A Chinese immigrant, Mr. Moy, recalled that "on the streets, every other man he met was a foreigner or a son of a foreigner in Chicago" (see Ting C. Fang's dissertation, "Chinese Residents in Chicago," University of Chicago, 1926). Researchers responded to the public pressure and concern over the arrival of immigrants into the city. Many claimed, then as now, that immigrants would aggravate existing problems and contribute to the deterioration of their community. Immigrants were often blamed for overcrowding, the rise of crime, delinquency, corruption, and for lowering the standard of living of the average worker.

Based on the utilization of the American city as a site to study race relations, researchers posed a number of interpretations. As social scientists abandoned the idea of the melting pot, for example, Robert Park provided a new interpretation of the "race relations cycle," asserting that immigrants experience the stages of competition, conflict, accommodation and eventual assimilation. Later, St. Clair Drake and Horace Cayton in *Black Metropolis: A Study of Negro Life in a Northern City* (New York: Harcourt, Brace and Company, 1945), asked the critical question: Is it possible for African Americans to ever achieve full equality?

Other scholars such as Humbert S. Nelli, Melvin G. Holli, and

Dominic A. Pacyga rejected the notion of Anglo-conformity and focused on the survival of ethnic communities such as Polish, Jewish, Italian, and Irish enclaves, which flourished in Chicago.

In the 1960s, social science models such as the internal colonial model developed by Robert Blauner argued that nonwhites had been colonized by white America. This model dismissed the compatibility of Europeans and nonwhite immigrants, arguing that the historical experience of nonwhites fundamentally differed from those of European immigrants. According to John Ogbu, groups such as Afro-Americans came to America involuntarily, faced economic oppression, political subjugation, and racism. Asians, on the other hand, were voluntary migrants.

Until recently, most studies of race have continued to address the successful incorporation of European immigrants and the failure of African Americans and other groups of color to do likewise. America's race relations theorists focused on Black-White encounters. Race problems usually meant "Black" problems.

The 1992 Los Angeles uprising revealed the complexity of inter-racial relations today. A different multiracial social reality requires radical approaches to address the structural issues of economic and political inequality, and issues of race and representation. For these reasons, many researchers are coming to Los Angeles. The city has emerged as the newest laboratory for social scientists as they begin to experiment and to develop new ideas about race relations.

I would argue that the 1992 unrest can be seen as a turning point in academic research on race, as the site has shifted from East to West. We chose to focus on Los Angeles as the site of race because of obvious factors such as demographic shifts, the changing political landscape, and the emergence of the city as a center for Pacific Rim trade. Indeed, L.A. is a metropolis in motion.

What does it mean to be a Korean American in the 1990s? Can Latinos set aside their regional and ethnic differences to form viable political action groups? Will African Americans continue to play a leading role in defining the tenor of race relations and the political agenda of those in City Hall? And what about other Asian Americans? What will be the future of the Whites—the numerical minority in Los Angeles?

With this volume, we invite you to join us in exploring a new site with a focus on racial relations that is no longer Black or White.

3

Jewish and Korean Merchants in African American Neighborhoods:
A Comparative Perspective

EDWARD T. CHANG

What has happened to non-African American merchants in African American neighborhoods since the 1960s? Many Jewish store owners fled from African American neighborhoods during the urban riots of the 1960s. "Jewish-owned stores were targeted by protestors, and many white owned stores were destroyed."[1] "And before August 1965 when the burning and rioting took place, most of the furniture and clothing, and a good many of the liquor and grocery stores in the area were Jewish-owned."[2]

Ethnic successionists argue that the Korean merchants in the 1980s and 90s have simply replaced Jewish merchants in African American neighborhoods and that Korean-African American conflict is nothing more than the "old" problem of Jewish-African American conflict.[3] They see ethnic succession as a "natural" or "proper" order in a multiethnic society. Competition for scarce goods, power, status and privileges leads to conflicts between different groups. According to this view, friction intensifies because Jews and Koreans seem to have "taken over" businesses in African American neighborhoods. Under these circumstances, African Americans resent Jews and Koreans who seemingly exploit them for their own economic benefits. It is important to note that as Jewish communities in the inner cities became transformed into African American neighborhoods, many Jewish merchants sold their businesses to Koreans who became the dominant group of merchants in these areas.

The purpose of this paper is to compare and contrast the Jewish-African American conflicts of 1960s with Korean-African American tensions of 1980s and 1990s. I address the following questions:

EDWARD T. CHANG is an assistant professor of ethnic studies at University of California, Riverside.

1) What are the similarities and differences between the experiences of Jewish and Korean merchants in African American neighborhoods?

2) Did Korean merchants simply replace Jewish merchants in African American neighborhoods?

3) Are there any differences in the patterns of inter-ethnic tensions in the African American community?

New Urban Crisis

Korean-owned small businesses in African American neighborhoods have increased rapidly during the 1980s. Since the middle of the 1970s, Korean immigrants have begun to fill the vacuum created by the departure of Jewish merchants and the relocation of large retailers to the suburbs.[4] Beginning in the middle of the 1970s, recent immigrants from Korea began to open grocery and liquor stores, vegetable stands, gas stations, laundry shops, indoor swap meets, and hamburger stands in predominantly African American and Latino neighborhoods. The influx of large numbers of Korean merchants into African American neighborhoods has resulted in increased complaints, tensions and dissatisfaction toward these merchants. Some residents have initiated "boycott" campaigns against Korean stores in Philadelphia, Washington, D.C., Baltimore, New York, Chicago and Los Angeles.

Although Korean-African American relations have deteriorated during the 1980s, relations worsened with the several highly publicized disputes involving Korean merchants and African American customers in New York and Los Angeles. The "Red Apple" incident in New York City in 1990 supplanted "Big Apple" as the symbolic term for the city. "Red Apple" is the name of the Korean-owned vegetable store that was boycotted by African American activists of the Brooklyn neighborhood of New York. Tensions had arisen since January 18, 1990, when a Haitian woman was allegedly beaten by the manager and employees of Red Apple, a Korean-operated store. Jislaine Felicine, forty-six, was accused by the manager of not paying the appropriate amount for the items she wanted to purchase. The manager, Chang Bong Ok, insisted that he and other employees did not assault the woman. Nevertheless, boycotts of Red Apple and Church Fruits took place during a year-and-a-half period.

In Los Angeles, two cases of disputes involving Korean merchants and African American customers further exacerbated relationships between the two groups. On March 16, 1991, a fifteen-year-old African American girl, Latasha Harlins, was killed by a Korean shopkeeper, Soon Ja Du, in South Central Los Angeles. This tragic incident generated anger, disbelief and shock from both communities. Several Korean-owned stores were reportedly attacked and vandalized by angry crowds.[5] At least one Korean-operated store had to shut the store down for six consecutive months to avoid violent protests by angry African American residents.[6]

Many Korean merchants called community crime prevention hot lines to express fear of retaliation by African American customers. The Koreatown police station reportedly received several telephone inquiries by Korean merchants who were burglarized and vandalized by African American customers. Korean Americans in Los Angeles hoped these incidents would not lead to the repeat of riots of 1960s. April and May of 1992 would prove otherwise. Korean-African American conflict has emerged as one of the most visible and volatile problems facing urban America today.

Bittersweet Encounter:
Jewish-African American Relations

Scholars have debated about the historical alliance between Jewish and African Americans. Are African Americans more likely to be anti-Semitic than Whites? During the 1960s, many concerned African American and Jewish scholars and leaders met to discuss the worsening relationship between the two minority groups. Katz, in his introductory remarks during Jewish-African American symposium, commented that it is now widely accepted as an incontrovertible fact that, "1) there exists a pronounced anti-Jewish sentiment among the Negro masses in this country, despite the active participation of many idealistic young Jews in the Negro struggle for equal rights, and the moral support given to the Civil Rights Movement by organized Jewish groups, 2) that Jews are reacting to this sentiment with an emotional backlash."[7]

To many Jewish Americans, anti-Semitism among African Americans is a troublesome phenomenon and difficult to comprehend since the Jewish American community has consistently shown strong support for the anti-slavery struggle and Civil Rights Movements.

Others dismiss the historical alliance between Jews and African Americans as a myth. They reject the notion that "African American-Jewish relations used to be good and now they have turned sour. The truth is, of course, that they never were really good."[8] Others have reinforced this sentiment: "while the Negro-Jewish relationships may have appeared to be peaceful in the past, it has always been tense below the surface, at least in the slums."[9] Even within the Communist Party, solidarity between Jewish and African American working classes never materialized. "In Negro-Jewish relations in the Communist Left there has been an intense undercurrent of jealousy, enmity and competition over the prizes of group political power and intellectual prestige."[10] Weisbord and Stein have defined Jewish-African American relations as a "bittersweet encounter" which fluctuated from cooperation and conflict depending upon different historical and geographical circumstances.[11] Marx also found that anti-Semitic feelings have not changed much among the African American population and that "they felt the same toward Jews now as in the past.[12] However, among those who reported a change in their feelings, the overwhelming majority indicated that this change has been in a positive direction."[13]

What is important here is the validation of anti-Semitism among African Americans. Anti-Semitism among African Americans is a special form of displaced aggression that targets their nearest competitor.[14] Reddick argued that "anti-Semitism among Negroes in the United States is a principally urban, northern and historically recent phenomena."[15] Of course, complex economic, social and ideological issues also underlie African American anti-Semitism.

On the other hand, some have argued that Jews and African Americans are natural allies because of their common historical experiences of racial and ethnic oppression.[16] These scholars deny or minimize the existence of anti-Semitic feelings within the African American community. "Thus, so far as I can recall, of all the anti-Semitic sentiments which have recently been publicized by the mass media, not a single one has come from an elected representative of the African American community."[17] Marx, on the other hand, found that anti-Semitism exists among African Americans, but that they are also less anti-Semitic than whites. "Jews were seen in a more favorable light than other whites by a four-to-one ratio" among African Americans.[18] Other progressive individuals and organizations stressed the historical alliance between these two minority groups. The Anti-Defamation League of B'nai B'rith reported that a five-year study of African American attitudes had shown African Americans to be the least anti-Semitic group in the country.[19]

Outsiders: Super-Achiever or Model Minority?

African American complaints about Korean and Jewish merchants have similarities. Korean and Jewish merchants are accused of being "money chasers," of "overcharging for inferior products," and of exploiting the African American community for their own enrichment. Reddick said, "add to high prices, inferior quality of merchandise—stale bread, tainted meats, storage eggs, defective furniture, second class dress prints, over-ripe fruit—under weight, penny short change and you have a community of irate housewives."[20] Other African Americans have echoed these complaints. "They all cheat." "They have to cheat 'cause we don't have nowhere else to go," African American women stated about Jewish merchants.[21] "The poor Negro's perception of a Jewish world is a very limited one: he knows little or nothing of Jewish culture, religion, or of the Jewish intellectual. Negroes do identify the Jews as the exploiting, cheating merchant who derives his income from ghetto dwellers, and takes it all out with him to his fancy home someplace else," according to Katz.[22]

Although African American customers patronize Korean American stores on a daily basis, the quality of interaction is superficial and shallow because of language and cultural barriers. Korean merchants and African American customers rarely come together to discuss each other's perceptions, complaints and problems. Unfortunately, it took the murder of Latasha Harlins to bring the two groups together to hold a "community forum" to air-out their frustrations and anger.[23]

Sometimes both Jews and Koreans are accused of planning to take over black neighborhoods:

"Koreans are buying buildings from Jewish owners which usually are run down buildings. Jewish owners can sell the building way above real value to Koreans, thus, African Americans have no chance of purchasing the buildings. . .Koreans increase rent to African American tenants, thus, kicking them out."[24]

Most stories focus on the economic (merchant-buyer or middle-underclass) aspect of Korean-African American relations that is often antagonistic.

Both Jews and Koreans are perceived as "super-achievers" or a "model minority." Indeed, economically and educationally, Jews and Koreans (Asian Americans) appear to have surpassed African Americans who have been here much longer. For this reason, the political demands of the African American community and the Korean or Jewish community differ. For example, while African American Americans are demanding a "minimum" quota in gaining admission to the universities and places of employment, Jews and Koreans (Asians) are demanding the elimination of "maximum" quotas which are used against them.[25] Shorris criticized the "new attitude" of Jewish community toward affirmative action. "When Jews were still on the left, Jewish interests meant social justice, human rights, peace, a world in which mercy prevailed; but as they moved to the right, the definition of Jewish interest changed, becoming more parochial, more direct. . .pursue their own self-interest to survive and proper."[26]

The myths of super-achiever or "model minority" tend to pit one minority group against another. Neo-conservative scholars blamed

African Americans for their failure to succeed in America by comparing the experiences of Korean or Jewish immigrants with African Americans. Why can't African Americans achieve as much as Korean immigrants, who have succeeded in a short period of time? However, this image of the model minority is simplistic, and grossly exaggerates the status of Koreans in America.[27]

Nonetheless, racial stereotypes promote antagonism, suspicion, fear and hatred. In this context, Jews and Korean Americans are blamed and scapegoated for the lack of economic and social advancement of African Americans. James Baldwin, in *Notes of a Native Son*, said "Jews are identified with oppression and are hated for it. Jews own everything."[28] In this context, it is understandable to hear complaints of African Americans that "Koreans own everything." However, only 10 percent of Korean-owned grocery and liquor stores are located in primarily African American neighborhoods according to the survey by the Korean American Grocery Association of Southern California (KAGRO) in 1989.[29]

On the other hand, Korean Americans are often viewed as "foreigners" who don't speak English. According to a 1988 African American attitude survey in Los Angeles, Asians are the least-liked ethnic group by Los Angeles African Americans.[30] "In New York, nearly 60 percent of Jews held some unfavorable stereotyped reaction toward Negroes and 70 percent of Negroes had some unfavorable stereotyped reaction toward Jews."[31] Korean Americans also hold negative views toward African Americans—"they are lazy," "they drink a lot," "they are uneducated," "they are low-class, dirty, and noisy."[32] Such negative stereotyping will further intensify and inflame racial tension.

Horizontal versus Vertical Relationship

Anti-Semitism among African Americans stems from landlord-tenant and employer-employee relations. African Americans disliked Jewish merchants who overcharged them, landlords who collected high rents, and teachers who controlled the lives of their children.

Korean immigrants, however, are primarily owners of mom-and-pop stores in African American neighborhoods. Koreans are not rent collectors, landlords, teachers or politicians. In this regard, the Korean-African American relationship seems to be far more formalized than the Jewish-African American relationship which often involved informal and personal contacts.

It is also important to understand the profound differences between the sociopolitical status of Korean and Jewish immigrants. Korean

Americans have never been a part of the so-called "establishment," (WASP) that has dominated the African American community for the past two hundred years.[33] Jewish immigrants have also encountered prejudice, discrimination and racism. Jewish immigrants could, however, become naturalized citizens of the United States of America and thereby defend their civil and political rights and privileges. On the other hand, Korean (Asian) immigrants were unable to defend themselves from racial hatred and discrimination. Defined as "aliens ineligible to become a citizen of the United States" until 1952, Koreans were denied naturalization rights.[34] As a group that were denied franchise, Korean (Asian) immigrants were historically excluded from participating in the mainstream society.[35]

African Americans were critical of Jews who were perceived as being part of a white America that had dominated and controlled every aspect of African American lives. Anti-Jewish sentiment among African Americans reflects hatred and anger toward white America. "African Americans are anti-Semitic because they are anti-white," declared James Baldwin.[36] Bender stated that "Negroes reacted to Jews as white men, as perforce part of the white majority, even if they were perceived to be different within that majority."[37] Many African Americans also saw practices of Jewish merchants as an extension of Jim Crow policy.[38]

African American is a racial categorization, but Jew is an ethnic classification. Korean is both an ethnic and racial term. What distinguishes a racial group from an ethnic group is that the "ethnic group results from inclusive and racial categories from exclusive processes."[39] Jews, as an ethnic group, can identify themselves as Jews but also have a choice to identify themselves as white if they so wish. Koreans, as an ethnic group, share a common culture, history and beliefs. However, Korean Americans can never claim to be part of white America because of the physical appearance that distinguishes them apart from Whites.

Wan Sang Han of Seoul National University defined *minjung* as people outside of the mainstream who suffer from economic exploitation and political subjugation.[40] If we apply this definition of *minjung*, nonwhites (Asians, African Americans, Latinos, and Native Americans) are *minjung* in American society. If the African American community is seen as demanding freedom from the economic, political, cultural and racial domination of white America, the Jewish group can be seen as part of this domination. African American-Jewish antagonism, perhaps, can thus be understood from the perspective of African American struggle for empowerment and liberation.

Because African Americans have been more actively involved in the Civil Rights struggle, they have gained more political powers and privileges than Korean or Asian Americans. The African American community has achieved significant political gains during the past twenty years. Mayors of two largest cities in California (Los Angeles and Oakland) have been African American. There are many state assemblymen, city councilmen, and other politicians who represent African American communities in California and other parts of the United States. It is noteworthy that a new Clinton administration appointed four African American cabinet members while selecting no Asian Americans to high-ranking government positions.

Moreover, Korean-African American relations is not rooted historically, unlike the bittersweet encounter of Jews and African Americans. Many African Americans have expressed solidarity with Jews for their common suffering and oppression in Europe (Nazi Germany) and in America. Jews were also active in the anti-slavery movement and the Civil Rights Movement of the twentieth century.[41] African Americans and Jews share a common history of struggle for equality and justice, and have developed mutual respect for one another. In spite of cooperation and alliances between the Jewish and African American communities, the relationship between the two groups has deteriorated since the 1960s.

The majority of Korean immigrants are newcomers who arrived in America after the passage of the 1965 Immigration Act. Many newcomers are unaware of the historical significance of the Civil Rights movement that paved the way for all Americans, particularly minorities. Since Korean American store owners in African American neighborhoods spend most of their time at work, they have very little contact with white America. Korean immigrants have a scant understanding of words like "prejudice" or "discrimination."[42] Thus, it is understandable that the perception of America by Korean immigrants is incomplete.

In sum, I view the Jewish-African American relationship as a vertical one, whereas the Korean-African American as a relatively horizontal one. Jewish-African American relations resemble the traditional Jim Crow South of economic, political, and social subordination of African Americans. The Korean American-African American relationship, on the other hand, is more horizontal because Korean Americans seem to have some economic advantages while African Americans have other political and social/cultural advantages. If this is true, it can be argued that Korean-African American relations is potentially the more explosive because members of each group view themselves as at least equal or "better than the other."

Exploitation versus Unemployment

African Americans have traditionally resented Jewish store owners who hired African Americans at low wages. This hiring practice was called a "slave market."[43] "The so-called "slave market" was the source of great antagonism. "In the Bronx, most of whose inhabitants are Jewish, Negro girls and women used to stand around at certain street corners where they would be hired for temporary domestic work at very low rates, and this practice aroused hostility toward the employers, who largely were Jewish."[44] The issue here is the exploitation of cheap labor by the Jewish employer.[45]

In contrast, Korean store owners are often accused of not hiring African American workers at all. During the boycotts of Korean stores in South Central Los Angeles between June and October 1991, a leader of the boycott, Danny Bakewell, of the Brotherhood Crusade, demanded that "all Korean stores in South central must agree to hire at least one African American employee."[46] Indeed, one of the major complains against Korean merchants has been the lack of employment opportunities in their own neighborhoods. African Americans also raised the concern that new Korean owners often fire employees as soon as they take over new businesses. African Americans remind Korean merchants that Jewish store owners at least provided employment opportunities to African Americans. On the other hand, African Americans believe that Korean merchants are excluding African American residents from jobs in their own neighborhoods. If Jewish merchants were able to hire African Americans, why can't Korean store owners also hire black employees?

Koreans express reluctance to hire black employees for several reasons. Simply, many Korean merchants cannot afford to hire anyone because many Korean-owned businesses are of the mom-and-pop type. These merchants must depend upon unpaid family labor as a source to generate enough profits. Korean merchants who are able to hire black employees complain that Blacks often demand higher wages. Other Korean merchants complain that African American youths are usually not reliable workers. One Korean merchant said that African American youths only want to work morning shifts. "I don't need help in the morning. I need someone to take care of the store in the evening and night."[47] For these reasons, many Korean merchants expressed their preference for hiring Latino immigrant workers. Korean immigrant merchants believe that it is easier to work with Latino workers who, as immigrants, tend to work hard like themselves. Language is another reason why merchants prefer to hire Koreans, with whom they can communicate.[48]

African Americans, on the other hand, perceive that Korean merchants are not really part of the community. They state that Korean merchants "don't contribute and participate in the community-based organizations." However, many Korean merchants have contributed quietly to African American commuity organizations.[49]

Of course, some Korean merchants refuse to make any monetary or other types of contributions to black neighborhoods. One of the reasons is because Korean-owned stores have a high turnover rates compared to Jewish-owned stores in African American neighborhoods. Since the primary motive for Koreans to open small businesses in African American neighborhoods is to make a large sum of money in the shortest possible time, they tend to sell their stores if the price is right. Therefore, it is difficult for Korean store owners to establish a personal relationship with customers. "It takes at least three to four years to understand a business environment and your neighborhood," said one Korean American businessman. "It is unfortunate that I must sell my business at this juncture. A new owner must start the process that I went through all over again."[50]

Unlike Koreans, Jewish merchants in African American neighborhoods maintained a "paternalistic" relationship with African American customers because many have lived and participated in the community activities.

Politics, Religion and Economic Threat

International relations involving homeland politics also have affected Jewish-African American and Korean-African American relations in different ways. The issue of survival for Israel often clashed with the Protestant and Islamic values of many African Americans. According to Richard Wright, "All of us African American people who lived in the neighborhood hated Jews, not because they've exploited us, but because we have been taught at home and in Sunday School the Jews were 'Christ-killers.'"[51] Anti-Semitism among African Americans was influenced by Christian culture that condones anti-Jewish sentiments.

The rise of anti-Asian sentiment has close ties with the increasing trade deficit with Asian nations during the 1980s. According to a poll by the *Los Angeles Times* (August 7, 1989), a majority of Americans felt that the threat of Japan's economic expansion was far more dangerous to America's national security than the expansion of Soviet communism. Anti-Korean sentiment stems from the fact that Koreans are perceived as "foreigners" who do not speak English. While Jews are perceived as a part of dominant white America, Koreans are seen as "foreigners" who do not deserve equal treatment as American citizens. Reflecting this growing "anti-foreigner" or "anti-Asian" sentiment, Los Angeles City Councilman Nate Holden introduced a proposal, "Stop Selling America," which would prohibit non-U.S. citizens from buying property in Los Angeles. Holden argued that "we are watching our precious land, a finite resource, being sold to foreigners to satisfy the greed of a few. . . . Our founding fathers never had intentions of selling out country to foreigners."[52]

Asian Americans are concerned about this resurgence of xenophobia that has its historical roots with the passage of the 1882 Chinese Exclusion Act. The act essentially prohibited most Chinese immigration to the United States and was the sole exclusion measure passed by Congress against a specific group. Throughout American history, Asian immigrants have often been scapegoated for the nation's economic and political woes. The passage of Foreign Miner's Tax (1852), Alien Land Law (1913), Immigration Act of 1924 and Executive Order 9066 (1942) are just some of the many laws and decrees that singled out Asian immigrants in an attempt to curb immigration or their economic and political advancement.

Asian Americans feel there are strong ties between the rise of anti-Asian bigotry and violence and the increase in America's trade deficit with Asian nations during the 1980s.[53] Loss of jobs, plant closures, and high unemployment rates in America are often blamed on the influx of imports from Asia. South Korea is one of the Asian countries that has recorded a trade surplus with America in recent years.[54] African Americans, who are usually the last hired but the first fired, thus blame Korean immigrants as the source of their economic problems. While the Jewish-African American conflict involved the political and religious issues around Israel and Zionism, the Korean-African American conflict is exacerbated by America's current economic problems, particularly the growing trade deficit with Asian nations. International issues often have racial and ethnic implications for different communities in the United States.

The majority of African Americans and Koreans are Christians. However, ideologies and beliefs of African American churches are quite different from those of Korean churches. Dearman found that more than 90 percent of Korean churches in Los Angeles belong to fundamentalist, conservative, or evangelical sects. Out of the sixty-five ministers who responded to the questionnaire, only one minister classified himself as a "liberal."[55]

On the other hand, African American churches are concerned with issues of racial oppression, discrimination and emanicipation. During the Civil Rights era, African American pastors and organizations including Martin Luther King, Jr. and the Southern Christian Leadership Conference (SCLC) played vital leadership roles. Churches continue their involvement with general welfare of the African American community today.

15

In sum, African American churches are more active in social and political issues than Korean American churches. Even theologically conservative African American churches still promote political activism and encourage their members to participate in voting drive or protest movements for example. In contrast, the theological and social concerns of Korean immigrant churches tend to be closer to more conservative white Protestant churches.

Furthermore, Korean immigrants came to America with blind trust in an "anti-Communist" ideology. In contrast, many Jews were sympathetic toward or active members of socialist or communist parties. Because many Korean immigrants are refugees from north Korea or a victim of the disastrous Korean War (1950-1953), they strongly reject thinking that has any connection with Communism or Marxism. In fact, many Korean immigrants identify labor unions as a communist organization because they were taught to believe that labor unions promote class interests. They are suspicious of any organization or group that promotes "class" interests because "class" often connotes "marxist" ideology.

The ideological conservatism of some Korean immigrants may make them reluctant to support social programs that are designed to help the poor, the uneducated, the impoverished and the under-privileged, such as welfare benefits, unemployment insurance, AFDC, or other governmental programs. On the other hand, liberal Jewish philanthropic organizations helped to support African American groups and their activities. In fact, Jewish participation in the National Association for Advancement of Colored People (NAACP) provided financial as well as moral support during the organization's early years.

As I stated earlier, because of these common interests and experiences, it was often unclear if Jews and African Americans were in fact allies or enemies. Uncertainty does not exist between Korean merchants and African American residents. There appear to be little commonality between the experiences of African slaves and their descendants and middle class urban Korean immigrants of 1970s and 1980s.

Conclusion

The Jewish-African American and Korean-African American relationships reflects the fundamental issues of economic exploitation of African American residents by Jewish and Korean merchants. Class is also a major element of interethnic relations as it involves the confrontation between the Jewish and Korean middle class and the African American underclass. Although many Jews struggled together with African Americans for the passage of the Civil Rights Act of 1964, they were primarily concerned with the elimination of *maximum* quotas set against them, while African Americans fought for the establishment of *minimum* quotas in employment, education, housing and political representation. Like Jewish Americans, Korean Americans (Asians) are also struggling to abolish *maximum* quotas set against them. Although Korean immigration is a direct result of the Civil Rights struggle of the 1950s and 1960s, very few Korean immigrants understand and appreciate the African American-led Civil Rights Movement.

In this essay, I have argued that Korean and African American conflicts of the 1980s differ from the Jewish-African American conflicts of the 1960s in many respects. The dynamics of the Korean-African American conflict occur within a rapidly changing domestic and international economic context. During the late 1970s and early 1980s, the American economy underwent profound economic, population and political restructuring. The U.S. economy has moved from a traditional manufacturing base to a high-tech and service-oriented economy. One consequence of this change is the widening gap between haves and have-nots, and the intensified oppression of African Americans. Feelings of hopelessness and despair are prevalent among residents of South Central Los Angeles.

Furthermore, I argue that it is unwise to compare Korean immigrants of the 1990s with Jewish merchants of the 1960s. Jewish Americans fought for and gained political, economic and social acceptance and equality in America. However, unlike African Americans, Korean (Asian) Americans still suffer from political, social and cultural subordination in American society, despite their legal inclusion in U.S. society. In other words, it is essential to differentiate Jewish American "success" with Korean immigrant "marginalization" as Korean immigrants are struggling with their status of "inclusion but subordination."

In my view, however, the possibility of building a coalition between Koreans and African Americans is greater than that of historical efforts to forge alliances between Jews and African Americans. One Korean merchant expressed his frank view of African Americans:

> In the beginning, I was afraid of African Americans and unable to communicate with them. African Americans are African Americans, thus, I did not have good impressions. Now, I feel close to them. I used to own a store in Pico Rivera (a predominantly Mexican area). When I saw an African American customer, I felt "*jung*" toward him. They are very kind, and some Koreans are worse than many African Americans."[56]

The possibility of forming coalitions between Korean American and African America communities appears more likely than an African

American-Jewish partnership. However, it will not be automatic. As Clark cautioned us that "it is naive to assume that, because Negroes and Jews are each in their own way oppressed and insecure, this will necessarily lead to a feeling of kinship and understanding."[57]

The possibility of a rainbow coalition will be a difficult task to accomplish. Unless there is a conscious effort by all groups, such a coalition will not take place. Korean American and African American communities must actively seek and create agendas and issues that will bond and strengthen both communities.

Notes

1. See *Report of the National Advisory Commission on Civil Disorders* (Washington, D. C.), March 1, 1968.

2. Shlomo Katz, ed., *Negro and Jew: An Encounter in America.* (New York: The MacMillan Company, 1967), 76.

3. See Howard Aldrich and A. Reiss, "Continuities in the Study of Ecological Succession: Changes in the Race Composition of Neighborhoods and Their Businessmen," *American Journal of Sociology* 81 (1976): 846-866; Daniel Elazar and Murray Friedman, *Moving Up: Ethnic Succession in America* (New York: Institute on Pluralism and Group Identity, 1976; Thomas Sowell, *Ethnic America* (New York: Basic Books, 1980); Herbert J. Gans, "Negro-Jewish Conflict in New York City: A Sociological Evaluation," *Midstream* 15:3 (March 1969): 3-15.

4. Many Korean immigrants purchased their stores from African Americans who bought stores from Jewish owners after the Watts riots of 1965. Since many Jewish store owners were anxious to sell their stores and leave the area, African American buyers bought stores at very low price. Beginning in the mid-1970s and into the 1980s, many Korean immigrants purchased small businesses from African American merchants. Therefore, African American merchants profited a great deal from this transaction.

5. For more information see the March 1991 issues of *The Korea Times English Edition* and *The Korea Central Daily,* March 22 and March 28, 1991.

6. Ironically, the owner of the burned-down store is Chung Lee, who has served as a co-chair of the Black-Korean Alliance.

7. For more details see Shlomo Katz, ed., *Negro and Jew: An Encounter in America*, 1967, vii.

8. Nathan Perlmutter and Ann Perlmutter, *The Real Anti-Semitism in America* (New York: Arbor House, 1982), 182-203.

9. Gans, 6.

10. Harold Cruse, *The Crisis of Negro Intellectual* (New York: William Morrow & Company, 1967), 169.

11. Robert Weisbord and Arthur Stein, *Bitter Sweet Encounter: The Afro-American and the American Jews* (Westport, Connecticut: Negro University Press, 1970), 65-84.

12. Gary T. Marx, *Protest and Prejudice: A Study of Belief in the Black Community* (New York: Harper & Row Publishers, 1967), 135.

13. *Ibid.*

14. Thomas Pettigrew, *A Profile of the Negro American* (Princeton, New Jersey: D. Van Nostrand Company, 1964), 44; Kenneth Clark, "Candor About Negro-Jewish Relations." *Commentary* (February 1946), 8-14; Harold L. Sheppard, "The Negro Merchant: A Study of Negro Anti-Semitism," *Journal of Sociology* 53:2 (September 1947), 96-99; George Eaton Simpson and Milton J. Yinger, *Racial and Cultural Minorities* (New York: Harper & Row, 1958).

15. Reddick, "Anti-Negroism among Negroes," *Negro Quarterly* 2 (Summer 1942).

16. Marx, 1967; Glazer, "Blacks, Jews, and the Intellectuals," *Commentary* (January 1969), 33-39.

17. Glazer, 34.

18. Marx, 135.

19. Fred Ferretti, "New York's Black Anti-Semitism Scare," *Columbia Journalism Review*, Fall 1969:21.

20. Reddick, 1942: 116.

21. Katz, ed., 76.

22. *Ibid*, 79.

23. Korean-African American tensions have been reported by major newspapers and magazines: James Cleaver, *Los Angeles Sentinel* (August 11 - September 1, 1983); Brenda Sunoo, *Rice Magazine* (April 15, 1985); *Los Angeles Times* (May 18, 1986); *Money Talks News* (March 15-31, 1985); *Insight* (February 9, 1987); *The Korea Times* and *Joong Ang Ilbo* reported Korean-African American tensions frequently during the 1980s and 1990s.

24. See *Metro News*, May 12, 1984; *The Korea Times*, May 30, 1984.

25. During the mid-1980s, Asian American community leaders charged the University of California at Berkeley and other higher institutions for imposing quotas against Asian American applicants. Finally, Chancellor Heyman of UC Berkeley issued a public apology and promised to take an appropriate actions to correct problems.

26. Earl Shorris, "The Jews of the New Right," *The Nation* (May 8, 1982), 556-561.

27. For further discussion of the "model minority" thesis, see Ki Taek Chun "The Myth of Asian American Success and Its Educational Ramifications" *IRCD Bulletin*. A Publication of the Institute for Urban and Minority Education Teachers College, Columbia University 15:1, 2 (Winter/Spring 1980); Asian Americans: "Are they Making the Grade?" *U.S. News & World Report* (April 2, 1984); William J. Bennett "An Education Success Story: making Something of Oneself" *Insight* (November 18, 1985); Bob Suzuki, "Education and the Socialization of Asian Americans: A Revisionist Analysis of the Model Minority Thesis *Amerasia Journal* 4:2 (1977), 23-52.

28. According to the Levine's study of "Who Owns the Stores in Harlem?," less than 40 percent of stores are owned by Jewish Americans. *Congress Bi-Weekly* (September 16, 1968), 10-12.

29. *KAGRO Magazine*, 1989.

30. According to the survey of African Americans in Los Angeles by Byron Jackson in 1988, only 62.4 percent of Los Angeles African Americans felt favorable toward Asians compared with 84.7 percent for Whites, 69.9 percent for Jewish and 83.7 percent for Hispanics.

31. Kenneth Clark, "Candor about Negro-Jewish Relations," *Commentary* (February 1946), 10.

32. For more information see Edward T. Chang, "New Urban Crisis: Korean-Black Conflicts in Los Angeles," Ph.d. dissertation, Department of Ethnic Studies at UC Berkeley, 1990; Ella Stewart "Ethnic Cultural Diversity: An Ethnographic Study of Cultural Differences and Communication Style between Korean Merchants and Employees and Black Patrons in South Los Angeles," M.A. thesis, Department of Communication Studies, California State University, Los Angeles, 1989.

33. WASP is an abbreviation for White-Anglo-Saxon-Protestant.

34. The Naturalization Act of 1790 designated only "free white" persons to be eligible to become citizens of the U.S.

35. Robert Blauner, *Racial Oppression in America* (New York: Harper and Row, 1972).

36. James Baldwin, "Negroes Are Anti-Semitic Because They're Anti-White" in Nat Hentoff, ed., *Black Anti-Semitism and Jewish Racism* (New York: Schocken Books, 1970), 3-12.

37. Eugene J. Bender, "Reflections on Negro-Jewish Relationships: The Historical Dimension" *Phylon* 30:1 (Spring, 1969), 64.

38. Louis Harap and L.D. Reddick, *Should Jews and Negroes Unite* (Negro Publication Society of America, 1943), 106.

39. Michael Banton, *Racial and Ethnic Competition* (Cambridge, Massachusetts: Cambridge University Press, 1983), 104.

40. Wan Sang Han, "Toward a More Relevant Korean Social Science in the 1990s: Bringing Living *Minjung* Back In." A paper presented at the annual meeting of Korean Social Science Association Meeting, 1991.

41. Bender, 56-65.

42. According to the author's own observation, the Los Angeles "riots" of 1992 was a wake-up call for Korean American community. See Edward T. Chang "America's First Multiethnic Riots" by South End Press, forthcoming.

43. Louis Harap, "Anti-Negroism Among Jews" *Negro Quarterly* 2 (Summer 1942), 105-111.

44. *Ibid.*, 106.

45. In Koreatown, it is a common sight to see many Korean American painters, gardeners, and builders hire Latino day laborers.

46. This was one of the ten demands made by Danny Bakewell of the Brotherhood Crusade against Korean American Grocers Association (KAGRO) during the negotiation to settle the boycott, November 1993. The author was personally involved in the negotiation process as a consultant to KAGRO.

47. Interview with Ha-In Kim, a liquor store owner of South Central Los Angeles.

48. Interview with Yang Il Kim, the president of the National Korean American Grocers Association (NKAGRO), March 26, 1991.

49. *The Korea Times*, January 7, 1992. According to the report, Korean Americans in Los Angeles contributed more than $100,000 to African American community groups in 1991.

50. Interview with Hee-Seung Choi, a liquor store owner of South Central Los Angeles. According to a recent survey of Korean stores in Southern California, the average length of ownership of liquor store was 5.6 years (1989), 4.37 (1990), and 3.46 (1991). See *Korea Times*, January 29, 1992.

51. Richard Wright, *Black Boy* (New York: Harper & Row, Publishers, 1966), 70.

52. *Los Angeles Herald*, June 30, 1988.

53. *Attorney General's Asian and Pacific Islander Advisory Committee's Final Report* (Sacramento: California Office of the Attorney General). December 1, 1988; *Plight of New Americans: Discrimination Against Immigrants and Refugees* (Los Angeles: Los Angeles County Commission on Human Relations, November 1985); *Hate Crime in Los Angeles County in 1988* (Los Angeles: Los Angeles County Human Relations Commission, February 1989); *Asian Pacific Americans: A Handbook on How to Cover and Portray Our Nation's Fastest Growing Minority Group* (Los Angeles: National Conference of Christians and Jews, Asian American Journalists Association and Association of Asian Pacific American Artists, 1989).

54. South Korea's economic success has been hailed as the "model" for third world countries. South Korea recorded a trade surplus with the U.S. in 1986 for the first time.

55. Marion Dearman, "Structure and Function of Religion in the Los Angeles Korean Community: Some Aspects." Eui-Young Yu et al., eds., *Koreans in Los Angeles* (Los Angeles: Koryo Research Institute, 1982), 165-183.

56. Interview with Youn-Ki Bae, an owner of an indoor swapmeet shop in South Central Los Angeles.

Communication between African Americans and Korean Americans:
Before and After the Los Angeles Riots

ELLA STEWART

As I walked through the quiescent streets of South Central Los Angeles last November 1992, I felt a sense of serenity that permeated the air. Except for a young African American female who stood at a nearby street corner waiting for the traffic light to change, the streets were devoid of pedestrians and traffic. From afar, all seemed well. However, upon closer inspection, remnants of last spring's riots prevailed in varied forms. Empty lots, boarded up buildings, and patches of lumber placed over broken windows of some of the remaining businesses were silent reminders throughout the city of the most devastating civil unrest in Los Angeles' history.

■　■　■

I initiated my present study in February 1992 as a follow-up study to my original 1989 survey of communication patterns between Korean American merchants and African American patrons in South Central Los Angeles.[1] My efforts, however, to locate and interview Korean American proprietors who had participated in my 1989 study on Korean/Black communication proved futile for the most part. As a consequence of the 1992 riots, I could only locate four of the twenty participants of the study. Many of the proprietors had either lost their

ELLA STEWART is instructor of speech communications at Los Angeles Trade Technical College and founder and president of Trawets Communications Outreach Program.

23

businesses during the riots, had set up businesses in other locations, did not have the necessary funds to rebuild, or had moved back to Korea. Other proprietors, those African Americans and Hispanic Americans who had suffered losses during the riots, also had relocated to other areas, begun to rebuild their businesses, or planned to rebuild pending availability of funds.

Upon completion of this survey one year later, the Latasha Harlins killing and the subsequent Soon Ja Du and the Rodney King verdicts served to reshape the attitudes of Koreans and African Americans in particular and the citizens of Los Angeles regarding interethnic tensions and hostility. During the months following the riots, my study was expanded and modified to include a wider population sample of the Korean and African American populations which reflected more diversified socioeconomic backgrounds.

As a researcher who had surveyed both groups from 1988 onwards, I was interested in how the perceptions and attitudes of African and Korean Americans had changed in the months before and following the riots. Among the general questions I had were:

—What were the general attitudes of African and Korean Americans toward the communication between them?

—What factors did each group perceive as causing interethnic tensions?

—What did each group perceive as solutions for solving interethnic tensions between them?

It is commonly argued that the sources of tensions, hostilities, and violence in Los Angeles are rooted in its changing ethnic, cultural, and racial makeup, leading to competition in employment, housing, and economic development among groups.

Koreans in Los Angeles are perceived to have advanced economically and numerically,[2] while the African American population has decreased in size and in economic gains. In Los Angeles, African Americans and Hispanic Americans trail Korean Americans in both educational and economic areas. The median family income for African Americans, Hispanics and Korean Americans in 1989 was $14,930, $15,531 and $20,147 respectively. Today, approximately eight million people reside in Los Angeles county and close to three and half million live in the city of Los Angeles alone.[3] In 1970, the population of the city was 71 percent White. By 1980, persons of African, Latino and Asian descent together were 51.1 percent of the total population.[4] By 1990, the largest ethnic group residing in the city consisted of persons of Hispanic origin (1,391,411). The second largest ethnic group consisted of persons of African descent (487,674), followed by persons of Asian descent (341,807) of which 72,970 are Korean Americans. Whites constitute about 1,841,182 of the city's population.[5]

While part of this economic disparity between African Americans and other ethnic minority groups can be attributed to a poor educational system and low income, part of the disparity can be attributed to racial discrimination. Thus the Soon Ja Du case not only symbolized fractured relationships between African and Korean Americans, but also demonstrated the differential treatment accorded to both groups by the American legal system. The civil unrest that followed the verdict in the Rodney King case on April 29, 1992 also underscored the differing perceptions that Koreans and African Americans had toward each other, and the difficulty of communication between the two groups.

Definitions of Terms

For the purposes of this essay, I want to broadly define a number of terms: discrimination, communication, culture, and intercultural communication.

DISCRIMINATION

Discrimination may take many forms but discriminatory practices can be divided into two main types: legal discrimination and institutionalized discrimination. Legal discrimination (overt practices) refers to discriminatory acts and policies that are endorsed by the law of the land. Institutionalized discrimination (covert practices) refers to discriminatory acts and policies that are not officially practiced or legally endorsed, but are nevertheless pervasive in major institutions such as schools, banks, and the courts.[6]

Institutionalized discrimination produces oppression. Turner et al.[7] define oppression in the following way: "Oppression is a situation in which a social system systematically and successfully acts over a prolonged period of time to prevent another identifiable segment, or segments of the population from attaining access to the scarce and valued resources of the system." First, oppression is a situation that endures over a "prolonged" period of time. Second, it involves "systematic" efforts of an "identifiable population"[8] to limit the actions of others. More clearly, oppression is a self-conscious process by specific people in particular contexts; it is not the unanticipated result of unconscious social processes. Third, such efforts must be "successful" if a situation of oppression is to exist. Fourth, because oppression denies access of one or more segments of a population to "scarce and valued" resources, it is a dimension of more general stratification processes in a society.

In American society, Black-White relations have historically involved relegation and confinement of Blacks to the lowest rank in the stratification

25

system, thereby denying them access to material well-being, power, and prestige. Similarly, in Japan, Koreans were typically discriminated against and regarded as inferior by the Japanese.[9] Oppression does not always lead to relegation to the lowest ranks. Some victims of oppression can be denied both power and prestige, but can occupy middle ranks in terms of their access to material well-being. For example, Asians in America such as the Japanese were initially denied access to power and prestige, but were allowed to accumulate wealth as long as their activities were confined to a limited range of roles. Jews in Europe until recently had been denied power but allowed to gather educational prestige and wealth from economic activities. (For a broad contextual overview of the histories of African Americans and Koreans, which is crucial to understanding the culture and attitudes of the two groups, see appendix 1 and 2.)

In America, while ethnic minorities in general are victims of some form of oppression, African Americans in particular are victims of oppression in almost every strata. In interviews, African Americans described "feelings of oppression" and "being victimized by the system" when citing some of the causes of the riots. "Feeling shut out" of the justice system and "being victims of double-standards" were other reasons African Americans cited as causes to rebel against the system, "not necessarily at Korean Americans."[10]

Korean Americans likewise stated that African Americans "suffer more racism" in America than Korean Americans "even though both are affected by built-in racism."[11] Although many Korean American appeared sympathetic toward the plight of African Americans, they were nevertheless angry with black riot participants and fearful of another civil uprising.

Both groups continue to blame each other for ethnic tensions and hostilities in Los Angeles and continue to offer prescriptive measures and suggestions on how the other should behave. In the 1992 study, however, many focused on elements within the American system that perpetuate racial and ethnic tensions and promote division among all Americans.

COMMUNICATION

Communication includes verbal and nonverbal interactions between two or more persons. Verbal communication is the use of "written or spoken" language to exchange messages, whereas nonverbal communication is characterized by the use of "gestures and other nonlinguistic devices" to send reciprocal messages.[12] Body posture, demeanor, eye contact, gestures, etc. are sometimes viewed by African Americans as the most important determinants of communication outcomes. This may be due to an old saying in the African American community, "Actions speak louder than words."

In Korea, it is often more important the *way* you do something than what you actually do or say. To damage one's *kinbun* may cut off relationships and create an enemy.[13] However, in the United States, Korean Americans focus first on what is said, followed by accompanying nonverbal cues during interethnic group communication. This may be due to the problems Korean Americans face in America interacting in a language that is difficult for them. Moving in and out of two distinctly different language communities becomes problematic for many Koreans as well as members from other ethnic cultural groups for whom English is a second language. In any case, what we speak and how we speak it are crucial factors in communication interactions in general, and in intercultural communication in particular.

CULTURE

Culture and communication are inseparable. According to anthropologist Edward T. Hall[14] culture is communication and communication is culture. The way we communicate, what we believe, what we say, the language system we use, the gestures we employ, are all a function of the culture we acquire. How we relate nonverbally to others is learned from the culture in which we grew up. How we dress, our use of time, the odors we savor, the distances we use to interact with others, and when, where, and to whom we maintain eye contact are all dictated by culture. Therefore, broadly defined, culture is the deposit of knowledge, experiences, beliefs, values, attitudes, meanings, hierarchies, religion, timing, roles, spatial relations, concepts of the universe, and material objects and possessions acquired by a large group of people in the course of generations through individual and group striving.[15] While cultural differences should be cherished and embraced, commonalities should be highlighted, for it is through commonalities that relationships are formed.

INTERCULTURAL COMMUNICATION

Intercultural communication is a process of transmitting and interpreting messages between culturally distinct peoples in which communicators may encode, perceive, decode, and interpret aspects of reality using conventions of meaning unique to their particular group.[16] Obviously, there are problems inherent in a situation where a message encoded in one culture must be decoded in another, since culture shapes the individual communicator and is responsible for the entire repertory of communicative behaviors and meanings we possess.

Thus, developing intercultural sensitivity and tolerance are essential in order to improve ethnic relations. Just as no two ethnic cultural groups are alike the same holds true for individual members within ethnic cultural groups.

Methodology

Even prior to April 29, 1992, the Latasha Harlins incident and verdict had caused tremendous strains between the Korean and African American communities. Between February and March, I had collected a small sample composed of random informal interviews with Korean American proprietors and African Americans in South Central Los Angeles in order to get a sense of the climate and "true feelings" of the two groups with respect to interethnic tensions and hostility. The attitudes from these informal interviews were similar to attitudes expressed in my original 1989 study.

In 1989 and prior to April 29, 1992, members from both groups felt that the behaviors and actions of the other group were inappropriate and were the cause of tensions. In addition, I noted from interviews that the negative attitudes of African Americans had intensified and heightened against Korean Americans as a direct result of the Latasha Harlins incident. African Americans were angry with Korean American proprietors and the justice system. They continued to criticize Korean Americans for their rudeness and disrespect. At the same time, they accused the Department of Justice of practicing double standards when African Americans were the victims or perpetrators of crimes.

Similarly, Korean American proprietors felt that African Americans were partially to blame for the outcome of the Latasha Harlins incident because they felt that black patrons showed disrespect, violence, and dishonesty toward Asian proprietors. Thus, each group held the other responsible for the tensions that existed between them.

After the April 29 riots, my research took on new dimensions. Research questions for the study and questions for the questionnaire were modified to reflect the attitudes of both groups from diverse geographic and socioeconomic backgrounds, as the outcome of the riots had touched and generated responses from persons from all walks of life.

A. RESPONDENTS

Respondents were a cross-section of seventy-nine African American and Korean American volunteers representing diverse geographic, socio-economic backgrounds (see table 1). The Korean sample consisted of 21 Korean American respondents: 8 Korean American proprietors who operated businesses in South Central/Southwest Los Angeles and serve African American patrons; and 13 Korean Americans (non-proprietors) from

Table 1. Demographic Characteristics of Respondents

Characteristics	African Americans (N=58)	Korean Americans (N=21)
Foreign-Born	8	21
American-Born	50	0
Number of Years in Los Angeles		
3-10 years	6	6
11-25	2	15
Age		
18-25	24	3
26-35	20	6
36-45	12	7
over 45	2	5
Education (College)*		
1-2 years	32	3
2-4 years	19	4
4-6 years	6	
Ph.D.	1	1
Sex		
Male	25	13
Female	33	8
Marital Status		
Married	13	16
Single	37	4
Other	8	1
Residential Area		
Los Angeles County	58	15
Orange County	0	6
Types of Business*	3	
Grocery Market		3
Liquor Store		4
Wig Shop		1
Number of Businesses Affected by Riots		
Completely Destroyed		2
Heavily Damaged		2
Minimal		3
No Damage		1

*Figure includes only eight Korean proprietors.

various occupational backgrounds. The African American sample represented 58 respondents: 48 students from an urban community college located in Southwest Los Angeles; and 10 African Americans from various occupational backgrounds.

Korean proprietors are defined in this study as owners of small neighborhood businesses located in ethnic minority neighborhoods in South Central/Southwest Los Angeles. Korean Americans (non-proprietors) are referred to persons in other occupational areas. A conscious effort was made by the author to include persons other than Korean Americans and African Americans drawn exclusively from South Central Los Angeles in order to increase the generalizability of the study in the following way: 1) reflect a sample made up of persons throughout Los Angeles who had interacted with members of the other culture in some context and who had been affected, in some way, by the riots; 2) to represent various points of view regarding the causes of tensions and hostility between Korean and African Americans.

Respondents were chosen for their self-identified membership in the following ethnic-cultural groups. Fifty African Americans identified themselves as either African American or Black. Eight persons identified themselves as Black and listed the country where they were born. For example, three of the Blacks were from Nigeria, one from Belize, one from the Caribbean, one from Ethiopia, one from Kenya and one from Trinidad. Length of stay in Los Angeles ranged from three-and-a-half to twenty-five years. Korean Americans (proprietors and non-proprietors) listed Seoul, Korea as their birthplace. The average length of stay in Los Angeles for proprietors ranged from eight to twenty-eight years. For non-proprietors, two to twenty years.

All respondents had some college background and had lived in Los Angeles two or more years. Although the level of education was not requested from the Korean American non-proprietors, all held professional positions. Korean Americans (proprietors and non-proprietors) residential geographic areas ranged from Koreatown to Orange County. African Americans residential areas ranged from South Central to Alhambra. African Americans ages ranged from eighteen to forty-five, with twenty-five males and thirty-three females. Thirty-seven were single, thirteen married, and eight were divorced or separated. For Korean Americans (non-proprietors) thirteen consisted of males and eight consisted of females. Four were single, sixteen married, and one divorced or separated.

Forty-eight African American students were employed in a part-time or full-time capacity, and eighteen were full-time students. African American professionals held positions ranging from computer analyst to contractor. Korean Americans (non-proprietors) held positions ranging from graphic designer to car salesperson.

B. DATA COLLECTION

Two forms of data collection were used: 1) survey questionnaire; and personal informal interviews (similar to free-response scaling method). Questions for the survey questionnaire were designed to elicit specific types of information from each group. The African American questionnaire contained twenty-six questions; the Korean American (non-proprietor) questionnaire contained twenty-eight questions; and the Korean American proprietor questionnaire contained twenty questions.

Close-ended questions elicited demographic data, the extent of intercultural interactions, the context in which communication took place and the frequency in which communication took place. The Korean American proprietor survey also included information on the location of business establishment, the extent of damage to business during the riots, the number of ethnic-cultural employees before the riots and the number of ethnic-cultural employees after the riots.

Open-ended questions were designed with the following goals in mind: 1) to determine what each group's general perception of communication between Koreans and African Americans before and after the riots was; 2) to determine what each group perceived as factors that contributed to interethnic tensions before and after the riots; 3) to determine the prevailing attitudes each group held about the other before and after the riots; and 4) to determine what each group was doing to promote positive communication and goodwill between Korean and African Americans.

Open-ended questions asked respondents to describe their attitudes toward communication interactions with members of the other ethnic-cultural group before and after the April 29 riots. Of the 58 questionnaires completed by African Americans (48 students and 10 professionals), two were incomplete and deemed invalid. Additional volunteers were secured. Of the 21 Korean Americans who completed questionnaires (8 Korean American proprietors and 13 Korean American non-proprietors), 3 Korean non-proprietors' questionnaires were incomplete and deemed invalid. Additional volunteers were secured. A Korean American assistant administered questionnaires to thirteen Korean American non-proprietors. Data from ten of these questionnaires were used for this study.

The African American sample was larger due primarily to greater accessibility and a greater willingness on the part of African Americans to participate in the study when initially asked. With the exception of the four Korean American proprietors who participated in the 1989 study, many proprietors were reluctant to participate in this study when first approached. However, once they understood the significance of the study, they were very responsive and offered a great deal of insight into the attitudes and feelings of the Korean American community regarding interethnic tensions between Korean and African Americans before and after the riots. Both groups spoke candidly of the causes of the riots, the outcomes, and what they planned to do to minimize interethnic tensions.

Although questionnaires were useful, they were limited in scope in that space did not allow respondents to discuss in depth their feelings about a particular concern. To compensate for this, an additional method, drawn from the "free response scaling" method, a respondent-based procedure, was used. During informal interviews, the author encouraged respondents to speak freely about any concerns they had after completing the questionnaire. The respondents, rather than the author, set parameters within discussions and controlled the quality and quantity of information. By using this method, the respondent was free to discuss anything that bothered him/her and draw limits whenever deemed necessary. The author ferreted through information gleaned from respondents "free talks" and established categories for this study, eliminating others. Primary and secondary categories were set up based on what respondents viewed as the direct causes of interethnic tensions and aggravating causes of interethnic tensions. Many statements made by African Americans and Korean Americans during "free talks" suggested that the lack of knowledge of the other group's history and culture may be a contributing factor to negative perception. Common statements included "Blacks should be more like Koreans, hard-working and religious," or "Koreans don't know what it's like to be oppressed."

Free talks allowed respondents to vent their frustrations and hostilities which were evident throughout interviews, and then reach a psychological state whereby positive discussions centered around promoting good will between African Americans and Korean Americans. For example, both groups spoke in angry or hostile tones of voice during initial and medial states of the informal interviews. However, over 70 percent of the respondents appeared more calm and hopeful when they discussed ways in which they would promote cultural appreciation and awareness.

Findings

African Americans in 1989 and 1992

In the 1989 study, African Americans had described the following as inappropriate behaviors exhibited by Korean American proprietors when they patronized Korean businesses: 1) being watched and/or followed; 2) having money snatched and/or having money thrown on counter; 3) being yelled at or spoken to in a negative way; 4) being accused of stealing; 5) being pushed to purchase unwanted items; 6) being refused to exchange merchandise; 7) proprietors made patrons' feel unwelcome in their businesses by not smiling or greeting patrons warmly, and 8) lack of respect shown towards patrons judgement and opinions. Additionally, lack of knowledge of culture and history were also mentioned as factors that contributed to poor communication.

In the 1992 study, African Americans again frequently mentioned the above factors as causes of interethnic tensions. A major portion of discussions, unlike 1989, centered on racism and discrimination in the American society, and their effects on African Americans. African Americans mentioned that institutional racism/discrimination were the major causes of hostility between Korean and African Americans. One respondent stated

> The existence of Koreans in our communities is not black people's major problem. The existence of covert and overt racism leveled against Blacks in particular is a major problem for black people because racism prevents Blacks from obtaining equal justice, equal jobs, and an equal education. Out of these frustrations come hostility, which ultimately leads to interethnic tensions.[17]

Another African American explained

> If Koreans showed more respect and courtesy toward African Americans on a daily basis when we patronize their businesses, chances are many of their businesses would survive a civil unrest because African Americans, in general, are warm-hearted people who want to like and respect Koreans. But in the present climate, African Americans are a very angry people because of past and present injustices in this country.[18]

Before the riots, thirty-one African Americans in my study viewed Korean Americans negatively and eighteen viewed Koreans positively. After the riots, sixteen remained positive toward Koreans and eleven changed their attitude from "negative" to "positive/negative." Six respondents changed their attitude from "negative" to "positive" toward Koreans. Only eight respondents changed their attitude from "negative" to "very negative" (see table 2).

The final questions on the questionnaire dealt with knowledge of cultural diversity, the culture of the other group, and their interest in learning about the culture of the other group. While fifty-three African Americans indicated that they had no knowledge of the Korean culture, twenty-eight indicated an interest in learning. Thirty indicated no interest

Table 2. African American Attitudes toward Korean Americans

	Before the Riots	N=58	After the Riots
Positive	18		16
Negative	31		23
Positive/Negative	9		11
Very Negative	0		8

in learning the culture and cited the following reasons: "I need to learn more about my own culture before learning about another culture" or "Koreans should learn the black culture since they come into our community." However, when asked if they were interested in promoting cultural awareness and appreciation between Korean Americans and African Americans, thirty-six indicated yes and explained how they wanted to go about doing it.

Many of the African American respondents who indicated that they had no interest in learning the Korean culture appeared to "soften" when asked what they were doing to promote goodwill between African Americans and Korean Americans. One respondent who had consistently talked about her negative feelings toward Koreans, along with racism in America, appeared to have a change of heart near the end of the interview. When asked what she was doing to promote cultural appreciation and awareness and goodwill among the two groups, her demeanor softened as she discussed how she planned to research the history of Koreans "because I want to know what makes them tick."[19]

Also significant is that most of the African American respondents who consistently viewed Korean Americans in a positive vein were from South Central Los Angeles. Those who viewed Koreans in a negative way were from Southwest Los Angeles and other geographic areas of the city. Another interesting finding is that many African American professionals described negative attitudes towards Koreans. One respondent stated the following:

> . . .It doesn't matter what my status is, how I'm dressed, when I go into those stores, some Koreans are just plain rude regardless of how courteous I am."[20] Another professional stated, "I could wear a jogging suit or a three-piece suit, I'd still be treated the same by some Korean

merchants as though I'm from Mars. Not all are this way, but some do not smile or greet me when I enter their businesses, and once my money was thrown on the counter—this was before the riots.[21]

African American respondents from South Central Los Angeles were generally more conciliatory and sympathetic toward Korean Americans. Many indicated at the outset of the questionnaire and/or interview that they held positive or mixed positive/negative attitudes toward Korean Americans and later discussed with greater enthusiasm how they would try to improve relationships between the two groups.

Korean Americans in 1989 and 1992

In the 1989 study, Korean American proprietors frequently mentioned the following behaviors exhibited by African Americans as inappropriate. 1) using bad language, 2) exhibiting loud and aggressive behavior, 3) shoplifting, 4) showing hostility when caught in inappropriate acts, 5) telling Koreans to go back to Korea, 6) exhibiting no shame and refusing to apologize when caught in inappropriate acts, 7) being accused of stereotyping all African Americans, 8) patron's refusal to pay for merchandise.

In the 1992 study, Korean proprietors frequently mentioned the following factors that create tensions and hostility between Koreans and African Americans: 1) violence, 2) exhibiting loud and aggressive behavior, 3) Latasha Harlin incident, 4) drugs, 5) African Americans' lack of education, 6) institutional racism, 7) lack of family values, 8) lack of education, 9) the welfare system, 10) lack of work ethics, 11) too many unmarried African American mothers, and 12) differences in culture and value systems. Koreans, like African Americans, viewed social elements in American society as major factors causing tensions and hostility between ethnic groups in America. Before the riots, Korean Americans (non-proprietors) frequently mentioned the following as causes of interethnic tensions: 1) differences in culture, 2) language, 3) different socioeconomic backgrounds, 4) different value systems, and 5) institutional racism/ discrimination.

While responses from Korean proprietors and non-proprietors were similar in nature, most Korean proprietors were more evaluative of African American behavior than Korean American non-proprietors and offered prescriptive rules of conduct for African Americans to follow. Korean proprietors frequently mentioned such statements as "More African Americans should be married so their children could learn family values," or "Blacks need to be more educated so they can refocus their energy," and "Blacks should be more like Koreans—educated."

Koreans and African Americans cited institutional racism and oppressive conditions as primary factors that contribute to interethnic tensions and hostility between Korean and African Americans. In the

1989 study, Korean proprietors and African American patrons viewed the behaviors of the other group as primary causes of tensions and hostilities.

Before the riots, fifty-six African Americans believed that communication problems existed between the two groups while eighteen Korean American respondents indicated that communication problems existed. It should be noted that both groups viewed communication problems and interethnic tensions as the same (see table 3).

Table 3. African American and Korean American
Perceptions of Communication Problems

Do you feel there are communication problems between
African Americans and Korean Americans?

	African Americans N=58	Korean Americans N=21
Yes	56	18
No	1	1
Somewhat	1	2

Most Korean non-proprietors were less inclined to offer rules of conduct for African Americans. Instead, they were very succinct in how they felt about factors that contribute to tensions and hostility. For example, if they were sympathetic towards African Americans and viewed them positively, some made philosophical statements like "Society has let them down, what do you expect?" If they viewed African Americans in a positive-negative or negative way, the statement might be "African Americans took out their frustrations and anger on Koreans—it's not our fault that they have problems in this country."

Before the riots, three of the eight Korean American proprietors viewed African Americans positively, and five viewed African Americans in a positive/negative way. For Korean non-proprietors, seven held negative attitudes towards African Americans with one positive/ negative attitude. After the riots, two Korean proprietors remained positive towards African Americans, and four remained positive/ negative. One respondent changed his attitude from positive to negative and one changed her attitude from positive/negative to negative. For Korean Americans (non-proprietors), two respondents maintained a positive attitude, two changed from a positive to positive/negative attitude, and nine changed from positive attitudes to negative attitudes (see table 4).

Table 4. Korean American Attitudes toward African Americans

| | Proprietors N=8 | |
	Before the Riots	After the Riots
Positive	3	2
Negative	0	1
Positive/Negative	5	4
Very Negative	0	0

| | Non-proprietors N=13 | |
	Before the Riots	After the Riots
Positive	7	2
Negative	5	9
Positive/Negative	0	0

Fifty-three African Americans in the sample had no knowledge of Korean culture, twenty-eight wanted to learn, and thirty were not interested in learning the culture. Eighteen persons out of the thirty felt they needed to learn more about their own culture before learning about another culture, and nine felt Korean Americans should learn African American culture (see table 5).

Only two of the eight Korean proprietors and three of the thirteen Korean non-proprietors had some knowledge of African American culture. While six Korean non-proprietors indicated an interest in learning the African American culture, only three had no interest at all in learning the culture. Of the Korean American proprietor sample,

Table 5. African Americans' Knowledge of Korean Culture		
	Know Korean Culture N=58	Willing to Learn
Yes	5	28
No	53	30

four respondents were interested in learning something about African American culture, while only one respondent indicated no interest. Eleven of the Korean Americans (non-proprietors) understood what cultural diversity means, while five Korean American proprietors understood the concept (see table 6).

Table 6. Korean Americans' Knowledge of African American Culture		
	Proprietors	N=8
	Know African American Culture	Willing to Learn*
Yes	2	4
Somewhat	1	0
No	5	1
	Non-Proprietors	N=13
	Know African American Culture	Willing to Learn*
Yes	3	6
Somewhat	1	1
No	9	2

*Note: Only for those who answered "No" to the question regarding knowledge of African American history and culture.

What is significant in this study is that the majority of the respondents wanted to learn something about the other culture.

Case Studies

Mrs. A

Mrs. A is a soft-spoken, forty-eight-year-old married Korean American proprietor, who owns a wig shop in Southwest Los Angeles and has been in the same location for over twenty years. She has a warm pleasant demeanor and is very religious. The author established a casual relationship with Mrs. A in 1988. Observations over the years revealed that Mrs. A, whose clientele consists of 99 percent African Americans, does not value her customers highly. She manifests this through evidence of lack of trust in long-term customers and by not hiring African Americans until recently, and a lack of knowledge of the African American culture which is reflected in the way she treats her patrons.

For example, earlier this year, the author observed the following: A patron of over fifteen years attempted to write a check for a product because she was short of cash. Mrs. A advised her African American customer that she could not accept a check for a particular item. The customer became irate and stated, "I've been coming here for over twenty years and you're telling me that because I'm short of cash today, I can't write a check?" Mrs. A replied, in her usually soft-spoken but firm voice, "No, you know I do not accept checks for that product." The customer and the owner argued for more than twenty minutes at which time the customer left, yelling she'd never return.

On another occasion, Mrs. A allowed her employees to handle a conflict with a patron even when the situation got completely out of hand. The patron wanted to exchange a product. The employee stated in no uncertain terms, "We can't exchange that product." The patron asked to see the owner. The employee called the owner, but Mrs. A who was standing upstairs watching and listening to the entire event, refused to come down.

It appears, after observing Mrs. A that, although she is a very nice person, she simply does not value her clients. She does not make long term clients feel any more important than short-term clients. This irritates many of Mrs. A's clients. The author offered Mrs. A the following suggestions: 1) hire at least two more African Americans since 99 percent of your clients are African Americans; 2) you and your employees attend a workshop/class on "How to deal with the public in a business context; 3) do not allow employees to settle disputes since you are on the premises most of the time. Talk to patrons and try to help solve the problem in a friendly, courteous way; and 4) try to make your long-term patrons feel appreciated.

Mrs. A agreed to try some of the suggestions. Several weeks after the riots, I stopped by to say hello. Mrs. A's business had sustained some damage but the damages were not as severe as other Korean and African

American businesses in the area. She had hired another African American. Now she has two African American employees. Additionally, employees appeared more courteous and smiled more than I remembered. Mrs. A remains ignorant though, on how valuable her customers are. She still refuses to offer check cashing service on some items to long term clients and does not adequately explain to patrons why she refuses the service. Also, Mrs. A does not learn long term patrons' names. However, Mrs. A is making gradual changes.

Mr. B

Mr. B. is a thirty-year-old Korean male who has operated a liquor store for six years in Southwest Los Angeles. He employs three African Americans in shifts. What is interesting about this Korean owner is that for the six years that he has been in business at the present location, he has employed all African Americans and these employees actually run the business in Mr. B's frequent absences. During the riots, Mr. B's business was guarded by employees and neighborhood people. Mr. B services over 90 percent African Americans. When asked why he has always employed African Americans, Mr. B stated "Nearly 100 percent of our customers are African Americans. It would be a slap in the face to the people who live in this community if I did not hire African Americans. And it's good for business."

Mr. and Mrs. C

A final example is that of Mr. and Mrs. C. For over ten years, this Korean couple operated a liquor store in the Pico area of Southwest Los Angeles. The clients consist of about 40 percent Hispanic Americans and 60 percent African Americans. Mr. C is a very nice person who has a pleasant demeanor but he is rarely in the store. Mrs. C, however, who serves patrons 70 percent of the time, has an extremely unpleasant demeanor. She rarely looks at patrons during transactions, never places customers' money in hand, but puts it on the counter and was observed many times arguing with customers who wanted to exchange a product, or who had accused Mrs. C of short changing them.

About two years ago, the author began to converse with Mrs. C. The communication began with a "hello" "thank you" and in time Mrs. C would smile when the author entered the store. We exchanged information about the weather. Finally, the author offered Mrs. C suggestions on how to improve public relations with her patrons and reduce tensions. She listened to the suggestions but kept complaining that the customers were always rude, and would steal if she did not watch them constantly. The author reminded Mrs. C that if she appeared more pleasant with customers that perhaps those patrons who exhibited rudeness would probably improve their attitudes. However, Mrs. C continued operating in the same discourteous manner. Many patrons stopped patronizing the business and began frequenting a Korean business four blocks to the west of Mrs. C's business. A married couple, in business about one year, operated this business and they went out of their way to be courteous to patrons. Though they had not been in the location long, many of the neighborhood people were often observed standing outside this business talking about how nice the couple was.

During the riots, Mr. and Mrs. C's business was completely destroyed by disgruntled patrons, it was later learned. However, the Korean business owned by the "nice couple" who showed respect toward patrons, was not damaged at all by the riots. One reason the business was saved is that neighborhood people guarded the business so that outsiders would not damage the establishment.

The above examples clearly show that skills in human relations and business ethics are essential in conducting business. While practicing these skills may not necessarily guarantee escape from damage during a riot, in cases where the Korean proprietor treats his patrons with respect and courtesy, the patrons will generally spread the word to others in the neighborhood, and will try to protect the Korean business if this becomes necessary.

Recommendations

Numerous recommendations and critical assessments have been provided over the years by community representatives, clergymen, politicians, academicians, students, professionals and the media regarding "what" African American and Korean Americans should do to improve interethnic relationships and "how" they should go about doing it. Organizations and city agencies such as Southern Christian Leadership Conference, the Los Angeles County Human Relations Commission, and the Asian Pacific American Legal Center have in the past and continue to work toward positive change by developing programs and projects that aim to enhance Korean/African American relations.

From a human communications perspective, the recommendations offered in the present study are to be viewed only as suggestions. The author does not attempt to offer a precept on how Korean and African Americans should conduct themselves in intercultural interactions. However, based on responses from Korean and African American respondents, and several years of observing communication between Koreans and African Americans as a participant-observer, I offer the following suggestions.

In the last ten to twelve years, there has been a major upsurge in racism, sexism and various other "isms" that affect in some way every American in the United States. Therefore, the question "How do we get along with each other?" applies to members of every ethnic and ethnic-culture group in America. To pretend that racism does not exist in America not only insults the intelligence of those who are victims of racism and discrimination, but worse, suggests a state of denial and ignorance on the part of those who question its existence.

Thus, the question "How do we get along with each other?" may necessarily need to include, "How do we get along with each other in the presence of institutional racism and discrimination in Los Angeles in particular and America in general?"

For African Americans and Korean Americans, the following recommendations, along with suggestions by Korean and African Americans are offered:

African Americans

Two out of three African American respondents indicated that they had no knowledge of their own true history and culture. In order to appreciate other cultures, African Americans need to learn more about their own history and culture. Therefore, it is incumbent upon African Americans to take the responsibility, and research the African American culture.

> 1)   Visit such libraries as the A.C. Bilbrew Library in Los Angeles which stores hundreds of books on the history and culture of African Americans.   Also, visit African American cultural centers which similarly offer a wealth of information on the history and culture of African Americans beginning on Africa's soil.   Knowledge of one's history and culture instills self-esteem and self-worth.

> 2)   Suspend judgements of Korean Americans based on myths and preconceived ideas.   Treat Koreans as individuals.

> 3)   African Americans choose to patronize whomever they desire. With this knowledge in mind, if an African American chooses to patronize Korean American businesses, extend to the Korean proprietor the same courtesy that you would want. Show respect for the proprietor and his/her business. If you find that a proprietor is rude or hostile, simply refuse to patronize the business. Just as all African Americans are not loud, hostile and violent, all Korean proprietors are not rude and hostile and cold. Another option is to patronize African American businesses in the African American community such as the "mom and pop" convenience store which opened last year in South Central Los Angeles to promote self-help and economic development in the African American community.

> 4)   Encourage positive communication with Korean proprietors about their culture and history, and share information about the true African American history and culture.

42

Korean Americans

Based on responses from many Korean Americans, some Korean Americans view African Americans in a negative vein based on myths and preconceived ideas.

MYTHS

* *BLACKS ARE LAZY AND DO NOT LIKE TO WORK*

African Americans created the tradition of hard work in America when they were brought to America as slaves. Slaves worked much harder than white slave holders. Even today, many African Americans work harder than other groups in America merely to survive. They are usually given the less privileged work assignments, along with less privileged hours to perform work assignments. Another significant aspect of the African American culture is that, in Africa, Africans had large devoted families and had the highest principles of humanity, respect for family, respect for elders, supreme confidence and intellectual productivity. Additionally, African Americans are among the most religious groups in America. Today, the effects of hundreds of years of servitude has affected the African American family with respect to family values, education and individual pride.

AFRICAN AMERICANS ENJOY BEING ON WELFARE

While some members of the African American community, just as in any other ethnic and ethnic-cultural group in America, take advantage of the welfare system, most African Americans work. Further, many would not be on welfare if they had job opportunities and equal pay. The African American is told to work, but oftentimes there is no job offered him/her. Fortunately, there are a number of job training programs now available to welfare recipients and other untrained African Americans to train and prepare them for careers.

AFRICAN AMERICANS ARE INFERIOR AND THEREFORE DESERVE TO BE TREATED IN AN INFERIOR WAY

This may perhaps be the most serious and damaging myth of them all because some African Americans, having internalized this myth, actually feel that they are inferior to the dominant society. Any group that is treated in an inferior way by a dominant group for hundreds of years will internalize these feelings, and some may engage in self-destructive acts as a result of these feelings. Many African Americans revealed during interviews that they had no real sense of who they were and no sense of their culture. Since self-esteem and confidence are largely derived from having a sense of who we are, African American parents will need to begin at an early age, teaching their children about the history and

43

culture of African Americans beginning in Africa. For older African Americans, it is incumbent upon them to go to such libraries and find books that explain the true history of the African American experience. African Americans can no longer wait for the public school system to provide an accurate account of their history. They must find these resources on their own. By doing so, young African Americans will eventually develop the pride and self-esteem that is needed to survive in America.

AFRICAN AMERICANS ARE JEALOUS OF KOREAN AMERICANS AND RESENT THEIR PRESENCE IN THE COMMUNITY

This myth has been perpetuated by the media. Many African Americans are angry with some Korean American proprietors by the rudeness and lack of respect shown them, but they are not jealous. During interviews with African Americans, many indicated that it did not matter who set up businesses in their communities, as long as the owners treated African Americans with respect and courtesy and helped the community in a positive way.

SUGGESTIONS FOR THE KOREAN AMERICAN PROPRIETOR:

1) Suspend judgements of African Americans based on myths and treat each patron as an individual.

2) Show courtesy and respect toward African American patrons.

3) Exhibit a pleasant demeanor when servicing African Americans (and other ethnic and cultural groups). This demonstrates to the patron that you appreciate his/her business, and minimizes tensions.

4) Obviously, the customer/patron is not always right. Thus, when conflict occurs, avoid yelling and/or threatening the patron. The owner, not the employees, should take the time and explain to the patron why he/she is being refused a particular service (i.e., exchange product, complaints, of being short-changed, refusal to accept checks).

5) Avoid ignoring the patron's complaint about a product or prices. Talk to the patron in a courteous manner with a soft, conciliatory tone of voice. Approaching problems in a calm manner reduces tensions and hostility.

6) Please remember, the patron is a human being, and becomes very hostile if he/she is made to feel less than human or if his/her intelligence is being underestimated.

7) Learn something about your patron's history and culture. By knowing something about the culture of your patrons, you will reduce tensions and hostility.

Interviews revealed that African Americans do not consciously single out Korean American businesses as targets for attack. However, African Americans did reveal that those Korean proprietors who were rude and consistently showed disrespect toward African Americans may unwittingly set themselves up for retaliation, especially during a civil disturbance.

Finally, to African Americans and Korean Americans, remember that both groups bring different histories, world views and styles of communication to communication interactions. For example, while the African American is more expressive in his/her style of communication, the Korean American is more restrained.[22] African Americans are extremely sensitive to how they are received in a communication context, specifically, the degrees of respect shown toward them, being recognized and treated as persons. African Americans are more assertive in some communication contexts and have a preference for directness and individual acceptance.[23] They have a greater involvement with humans than with objects. Further African Americans are more likely than most ethnic and cultural groups to detect superficiality in a communication interaction, whether they acknowledge its presence or not.

On the other hand, Korean Americans are more restrained in communication interactions. To the Korean, the most important thing to an individual is recognition of his "selfhood." The state of inner feelings, his/her prestige, his/her awareness of being recognized as a person, and his/her face or self-esteem are a part of his/her *kibun* (mood). When the KIBUN is good, the Korean feels good. Keeping the *kibun* in good order often takes precedence over other considerations. For many Koreans, it is often more important to feel right than to be right if a choice must be made. Koreans, like Asians in general, prefer a more formal and distinct relationship through predictable behavior and small amounts of openness.[24] Intimacy and openness are traditionally reserved for the family. The Confucian philosophy influences Koreans' behavior. For the Korean, the wise man is often considered to be one who can make things appear in such a way that all will feel at peace, comfortable and secure.

Conclusion

While this study attempted to "find out" what were the prevailing attitudes of Korean and African Americans with respect to factors that contribute to interethnic tensions, it also attempted to provide a way for African Americans and Korean Americans to "open up" and release some of the tensions and hostility by communicating their true feelings about any aspect of relations between African Americans and Korean Americans.

The study served this purpose in the following way: I was privy to various emotions of the respondents as they discussed what and why they felt the way they did about relations between Korean and African Americans. It was only after respondents had vented their feelings that they were able to speak of positive relationships with members of the other group based on positive efforts they would make to promote good will.

While this study does not provide all the answers to improved relations between ethnic and ethnic cultural groups, it might be useful as a reference and guide when studying intra- and interethnic communication. Edward Hall, anthropologist, once said "Most behaviors in intercultural interactions do not spring from malice but from ignorance. We are not only ignorant of what behaviors are expected from others, but we are equally ignorant of what we are communicating to other people by our own normal behavior." It is the responsibility of every American regardless of race, creed, religion, culture, to become sensitive to the way in which our fellow neighbors are receiving our verbal and non-verbal messages.

The social ills in our society such as institutional discrimination against ethnic culture groups, women, the aged, will not erase themselves. Every member in the American society will need to do its fair share to promote good will and understanding among all groups. In the meantime, to reiterate the sentiments of African American and Korean American participants of this study, we can begin to improve interethnic relations in Los Angeles and across America by 1) showing common courtesy and respect for our neighbor; 2) by valuing and treating each person as a unique human being from a unique history/culture and deserving of the same fundamental rights as you would want for yourself; and 3) by showing respect for the other's differences while searching for the one thread of commonality that can promote positive communication and good will among all people.

Finally, one Korean American concluded her interview with the following: "Please tell the readers of this study that in the future there should never, never, never be another riot. It hurt too many people. We must open up to one another—we must talk—we must get along!"

Appendix I.

OVERVIEW OF THE HISTORY OF AFRICAN AMERICANS AND KOREAN AMERICANS
AFRICAN AMERICANS

An Afrocentric perspective on the African American's social reality starts with recognition of an African past[25] and considers the complexities of life in a segregated America and the elements that fundamentally shape peoples' lives. In doing so, one can examine the dynamics that constitute a struggle to balance culture and class in the context of an environment replete with institutionalized racism and discrimination.

While other ethnic and ethnic cultural groups migrated to America to share in the American dream, a vision that promised upward mobility, and the freedom to pursue life, liberty, and the pursuit of happiness, African Americans were captured by Europeans, placed in bondage and catapulted into a life of servitude. The Europeans came to America in search of a new and more complete freedom; the Africans came because the last vestige of their freedom had been taken away; the Europeans came in search of new ways of exploring the full potential of their humanity, the Africans came under conditions which denied even their basic humanity.[26]

For the Europeans, America was to be a land of the free, where the self-evident truth of human equality was to be sufficient ground for individual liberty and universal justice.[27] For the African, America was to mean over two hundred years of slavery, for which after that would come a far too late discovery that even with freedom, there would be social and moral factors with respect to the African American's place in American society, which would qualify, define and redefine that freedom for the rest of his/her life.

INSTITUTIONALIZED SLAVERY IN AMERICA

The first African slaves were brought to Virginia in the mid-seventeenth century. Before 1661 Africans were not true slaves because they were listed in the early census counts as indentured servants for whom manumission after a period of servitude was common. By 1661 and 1662, however, the Virginia Assembly passed legislation that made Africans slaves for life and dictated that children born to them in the new world would also be enslaved for life. A demand for cheap labor which led to massive slave trade ultimately brought some 400,000 Africans to America.[28]

While resilience is a major characteristic of African Americans, such resilience takes its toll over hundred years of servitude. The history of the African American has been one of sustained oppression, discrimination, and denial of basic civil rights and human dignity.

The myth of their racial inferiority—their irresponsibility, promiscuity, laziness, and lower intelligence was assiduously propagated as a justification for their continued subjugation.[29]

Although slavery was "legally" ended over a hundred years ago, the over three hundred years of brutality and unnaturalness have gravely impaired African Americans in general and African American males in particular.[29] This enslavement was so destructive to the natural life process that current generations of African Americans, though five or six generations removed from the actual experience of slavery, still carry the scars of this experience in their social and mental lives.[30]

According to Madhubuti[31], one of the tragedies of black life in America is that many African Americans never acquire insight into their own existence, "They just do not know who they are and this confusion about identity and source is at the core of black people's problems." Blacks are the product of a slave history, and Eurocentric world view that by definition cannot be developmental or inspirational. This history, for the most part, has been written and disseminated by Europeans from a European perspective and serves as a frame of reference for others to judge and value the worth of the African American.

According to Akbar,[32] "slavery is the modern genesis experience of Africans in the Western world." Contained in this genesis is much about the continued social, economic, political, and cultural reality of African Americans. "There is contained in this tragic drama, the nucleus of a mind wrought with the agonies of oppression of the most inhuman form."[33]

Korean Americans, like African Americans, also share a history of oppression.

Appendix II.

KOREAN AMERICANS

Like African Americans, Korean Americans have surmounted over-whelming odds to overcome their long history of oppression under foreign rule. Although Koreans have had long periods of stable self-government, they have lived at times under rule from China, Japan, the Soviet Union and the United States. In spite of this, Koreans have maintained a distinct cultural and political identity.

Among some ethnic groups, coping mechanisms are developed to pyschologically handle life's struggles and tragedies. For example, the old saying, "It bees dat way sometimes,"[34] though not grammatically correct according to the American English structure, is used by many African Americans to describe a condition that occurs habitually. Similarly, for Koreans, the term *han* refers to a released energy which drives them to work with a kind of frenzy, to get an education, be adaptable, disciplined and sacrifice themselves for the betterment of their families and country.[35]

HISTORICAL PERSPECTIVE

For centuries, political and religious leaders kept the people of Korea under a giant lid that prevented them from developing their potential. They were like "steel springs pressed nearly flat with no way to release their energy, curiosity or creativity."[36] The repressed energy, repressed needs, and aspirations of the Koreans over five thousand years, is what make up the psyche force that motivates and energizes them.[37] Like African Americans, Koreans are resilient people. One of their virtues is their ability to endure hardship and bounce back.

From ancient periods, Korea had close ties with China and China exerted great influence on Korea's politics and culture. While Koreans genuinely respected China's great civilization, the relationship between the two countries was also a means of ensuring Korea's existence and independence. For the Chinese, befriending Korea was a good way of guaranteeing tranquility in the neighboring countries where its power did not reach. Their relationship was cemented by the Confucian notion of duties and obligations, and served the interest of both parties. The bond lasted for centuries without much stress. In the cultural realm, Buddhism, Confucianism and the civil service examination system were all imported from or through China. Hence, the Korean culture was similar in many ways to that of China.[38]

Korea lost respect for China in the latter part of the nineteenth century when it tried to convert their traditional Confucian relationship into a naked imperial colonial one and turn Korea into a Chinese colony. To the Korean, China became just another chauvinistic power that took advantage of Korea's weakness. Consequently, few Koreans bemoaned Chinese defeat in 1895 by the Japanese.[39]

With only two hundred kilometers between their nearest points, the Korean and Japanese people have had extensive contact since the beginning of their histories. As in the case in many relationships among close neighbors, the two peoples have not always enjoyed friendship. The Korean participation in Kublai Khan's abortive invasions of Japan in 1274 and 1281 did not enhance Korean-Japanese relationships. Hideyoshi's invasion of Korea between 1592 and 1598 devastated much of southern Korea, evoking bitter memories for a long time afterward. But the Tokugawa regime (1603-1868) in Japan actively sought friendly relations with Korea, and the Koreans dispatched twelve friendly missions to Japan between 1607 and 1811. Both countries were deeply imbued with Confucianism (an ethical doctrine that governs human relationships and behaviors) at that time, and this affinity served as a bond between the two equals.[40]

The encroachment of the West in East Asia since the eighteenth century gravely affected the relationship between the two peoples. Japan not only sought to strengthen itself by emulating the West but decided on continental expansion as a means of strengthening itself against Western aggression. Korea became Japan's first step toward the continent. In spite of its long and proud history, Korea was not able to fend for itself; she and her people were forced to suffer humiliation at the hands of Japan. The reasons for this are manifold. By the end of the nineteenth century, the Yi Dynasty was at the end of its dynastic cycle. Because the powerful families and Confucian academies did not pay tax in spite of their huge land holdings, the state was impoverished. The peasantry, constituting over 90 percent of the population, had to bear the brunt of the corrupt system, and many of them simply fled their farms.

Korea at this time was monolithic, rigid, self-righteous and exclusive. Its doors had been closed to all foreign countries for three hundred years, except for China and occasionally Japan.

Secure in the knowledge of Confucianism, the Korean literati rejected any idea that contradicted what they believed to be the truth. The prevailing orthodoxy could not be questioned or changed without a calamity. It was a proud, dogmatic and closed society that continued on in spite of itself. Soldiers were held in low esteem, and the literati neglected national defense.

The Yi Dynasty was doomed to fall but before the Koreans themselves could reset the course, the Japanese intervened.

During the 1880's Japan and China became rivals in Korea, which was controlled by China. The rivalry led to the Chinese-Japanese war of 1894-1895. Japan won and China was forced to give up its claim on Korea. Japan annexed Korea in 1910 and turned it into a colony. Generations of Koreans who lived under Japanese colonialism look back to those thirty-five years of Japanese rule with anger and disgust. The Japanese plundered resources and humiliated the Koreans by attempting to erase all Korean identity.

Under Japanese occupation, Koreans were strongly pressured to conform to Japanese standards. The Korean language was prohibited in the schools and in public use. The teaching of Korean history and culture was forbidden. Koreans were required to take on Japanese names, and the program of full integration of the Korean peninsula into the Japanese Empire was greatly accelerated. During the period of Japanese occupation, Koreans were allowed to hold only subordinate positions in government. They were used as cheap labor for Japan's industrial development. Thus, Koreans came to resent their second-class citizenship in their own country.

In the 1930s and 1940s, the Japanese also exhausted the Koreans, both physically and mentally, by pushing them to serve the cause of the Japanese empire in its holy war against the United States, Britain and allies. They governed Korea chiefly to benefit their own interests. Japanese, among other atrocities toward Koreans, took their land and sold it to Japanese settlers. Korea, thus, remained a Japanese colony oppressed and her people denied alienable rights until 1945 at which time Japan was defeated in World War II.

Labeled as one of the bloodiest wars in history during that period, the 1950 Korean war, which stemmed from boundary control, was deemed the first war in which a world organization—the United Nations—played a military role. The war ended in 1953 when a truce was signed.

Subsequent involvement by the U.S. and Russia resulted in U.S. occupation of the southern half of Korea (South Korea), with Russian forces occupying the northern half of Korea (North Korea).

Korea's lengthy history of territorial, political and human rights struggle left its people worn and its economy frail. During the three-year war, Korean families were torn apart and since 1950 could not see each other. Only in 1972 did North and South Korea begin to talk to each other, but the tensions have not dissipated.

In September, 1985, thirty-five persons from the South and thirty from the North crossed the parallel to embrace momentarily their long lost family members, but it has been impossible to arrange such a visit since that time.

Today, South Korea has changed significantly. Its phenomenal growth since the late 1960s is due largely to the export-oriented industrial policy adopted by President Park Chung Hee, president from 1963-1979.[41]

The rapid economic development brought about a profound change in the attitude of its people. The two decades of success gave the people a confidence they had lacked. It also renewed the pride the people once had about their country. But Koreans remain identifiably Korean in their basic attitudes and behaviors. The family, a basic unit of society, provides a key to understanding Koreans. Korean people have attached so great an importance to the family that they have considered the society as an extended family. The mode of behavior of a family may easily be applied to that of their social life.[42] The Korean society is organized on an intricate network of personal connections, it is still an authoritarian hierarchy. People still resort to ritualistic face-saving facades and emphasize class and rank.[43]

Thus, it is against the backdrop of Confucianism, a strict hierarchal society, decades of suffering and anguish at the hands of foreign powers, and internal political and economic strife, that one must view the Korean history and culture.

Similarly, the African American can only be understood from an Afrocentric perspective against the backdrop of the pre-shores of Africa, their bondage in America, and the effects that such bondage produced spiritually and psychologically.

Notes

The author wishes to thank Helen Kyung Park, Cinda McKinney and Professors Thurman Robinson, Dorien Grunbaum and Lorraine Megowan of Los Angeles Trade Technical College for their support and assistance; and special thanks to the African American and Korean American participants of this study.

1.   Ella Stewart, "Ethnic Cultural Diversity: An Interpretive Study of Cultural Differences and Communication Styles between Korean Merchants/Employees and Black Patrons in South Los Angeles," M.A. thesis, California State University, Los Angeles, Department of Communication Studies, 1989.

2.   Eui-Young Yu, Earl H. Phillips, and Eun Sik Yang, *Koreans in Los Angeles: Prospects and Promises* (Los Angeles: Center for Korean-American and Korean Studies, California State University, 1982).

3.   U.S. Bureau of the Census (Washington, D.C., 1990).

4.   U.C.L.A. Ethnic Studies Centers, *Ethnic Groups in Los Angeles: Quality of Life Indicators* (1987).

5.   U.S. Bureau of the Census.

6.   Michael McKee and Ian Robertson, *Social Problems* (New York: Random House, Inc., 1975).

7.   Jonathan H. Turner, Royce Singleton, and David Musick, *Oppression: A Socio-History of Black-White Relations in America* (Chicago: Nelson Hall, 1984).

8.   *Ibid.*, 3-4.

9.   *Ibid.*, 4.

10. Author's interviews with African Americans, May-November 1992.

11. Author's interviews with Korean Americans, May-November 1992.

12. Larry A. Samovar and Richard E. Porter, and Nemi C. Jain, *Understanding Intercultural Communication: A Reader* (Belmont, California: Wadsworth, Inc., 1982)

13. Paul Crane, *Korean Patterns* (Seoul, South Korea: Taewon Publishing Company, 1978).

14. Edward T. Hall, *Beyond Culture* (Garden City, New York: Doubleday & Company, 1976), 9-25.

15. Nancy F. Burroughs, Patricia Kearney, Timothy Plax and Melvin L. DeFleur, *Mastering Communication in Contemporary America* (Mountain View, California: Mayfield Publishing Company, 1993), 110-111.

16. *Ibid.*, 111.

17. Author's interviewee.

18. *Ibid.*

19. *Ibid.*

20. *Ibid.*

21. *Ibid.*

22. Mary Jane Collier, Intercultural Communication Competence and Negotiation of Cultural Identities, paper presented at the Speech Communication Association Conference, November 1988, New Orleans, Louisiana.

23. MICHAEL L. Hecht, Mary Jane Collier, and Sidney A. Ribeau, *African American Communication: Ethnic Identity and Cultural Interpretation* (Newbury Park, California: Sage Publications, 1993), 102.

24. Collier, 1988.

25. Molefi K. Asante, *Afrocentricity: The Theory of Social Change* (Buffalo, New York: Amulefi Publishing Company, 1980), 2-3.

26. C. Eric Lincoln, *The Negro Pilgrimage in America* (New York: Bantham Pathfinders, 1967), 2.

27. *Ibid.*, 3.

28. *Ibid.*, 2-3.

29. Haki R. Madhubuti, *Black Men: Obsolete, Single, Dangerous? The African American Family in Transition* (Chicago: Third World Press, 1990).

30. Stanley Guterman, *Black Psyche, the Model Personality Patterns of Black Americans* (New York: The Glendessary Press, 1972).

31. Madhubuti, 4.

32. Na'im Akbar, *Chains and Images of Psychological Slavery* (Jersey City, New Jersey: New Mind Productions, 1984).

33. *Ibid.*, 1.

34. Geneva Smitherman, *Talkin and Testifying: The Language of Black America* (Boston: Houghton-Mifflin Company, 1977), 16-34.

35. Boye De Mente, *Korean Etiquette & Ethics in Business* (Lincolnwood, Illinois: NTC Business Books, 1988), xi.

36. Chong Sik Lee, *Korea: The Land of the Morning Calm* (New York: Universe Books, 1988).

37. *Ibid.*

38. *Ibid.*

39. *Ibid.*

40. *Ibid.*

41. Chun Shin-Yong, *Korean Society* (Seoul, South Korea: International Cultural Foundation, 1976), 69.

42. Hong Yi-Sup, *Korea's Self-Identity* (The Republic of Korea: Yonsei University Press, 1973).

43. Crane, 13-26.

Asian Americans and Latinos in San Gabriel Valley, California:
Ethnic Political Cooperation and Redistricting 1990-92

Leland T. Saito

After the racial turmoil of the 1960s and 1970s, the relative calm of the 1980s seemed to indicate that the United States was entering a period of improved race relations. However, the racial rhetoric of politicians such as Jesse Helms, the popularity of ex-Ku Klux Klan member David Duke in the Louisiana elections, and the rise in racial hate crimes once again brought race and ethnic relations to the forefront of public attention. In addition to the conflicts of Anglos versus African Americans that have long dominated the discourse on race and ethnic relations, conflict between ethnic groups, such as Korean small business owners and their African American clientele, have now emerged.

Interethnic struggle reached a high point following the acquittal of the four Los Angeles police officers accused of using violent force against Rodney King, an African American. Following the verdict, hundreds of businesses owned by Koreans and other ethnic groups were looted and burned down by African Americans and Latinos.

Against this backdrop of racial tension, I examine political relationships between Asian Americans and Latinos in the San Gabriel Valley, located in Los Angeles County. I examine an Asian American organization that was established around the issue of redistricting and reapportionment and how the group formed an alliance with its Latino counterpart in the region. In this case, the Asian American and Latino organizations were able to reach agreement on plans that accomplished the complex task of protecting the political interests of Latinos and Asian Americans.

LELAND T. SAITO is assistant professor in the Ethnic Studies Department and Urban Studies and Planning Program at the University of California, San Diego.

55

What were the circumstances in the San Gabriel Valley that led to cooperation in the redistricting process between Asian Americans and Latinos? The Asian American and Latino communities overlap in the region so that district plans would affect both groups.

The San Gabriel Valley is an ideal place to study ethnic relations because of its demographics. Beginning in the 1970s, the formerly Anglo population experienced rapid change when large numbers of Asian Americans and Latinos entered the region. For example, Monterey Park has become the first city outside of Hawaii with a majority (57.5 percent) Asian American population.[1] At the regional level, Latinos have become the majority population in the valley and they hold all elected state and federal offices that cover Monterey Park. Yet, vestiges of Anglo political dominance remain on the local level in the form of Anglo control of some city councils.

This study primarily uses data from ethnographic fieldwork and interviews collected from 1990 to 1992. Census and voter registration data were also utilized. Ethnographic fieldwork was critical for documenting and analyzing events emerging from the historical and contemporary factors that formed the context for ethnic relations in the San Gabriel Valley.

This paper differs in three ways from other studies in race and ethnic relations. First, community studies traditionally examine one ethnic group, or compare an ethnic group with Anglos; this study examines two groups, Asian Americans and Latinos.[2] Second, most studies examining ethnic relations examine conflict,[3] whereas my research examines the circumstances around the volatile process that led to ethnic cooperation rather than conflict. Third, while one school of thought suggests that ethnicity is decreasing in importance politically, my study supports the persistence of ethnicity in politics.

Theoretically, one school of thought suggests that economic class is increasing in importance with a relative decline in ethnicity. Milton Gordon, in his formulation of assimilation theory, believed that ethnicity, "defined or set off by race, religion, or national origin," was a temporary condition which would disappear as groups "assimilated" into the mainstream.[4] In politics, Robert Dahl focused on the overlap of generation and economic class, concluding that ethnic politics would lose its meaning when an ethnic group made the transition from an immigrant group which is economically homogeneous to the third generation which becomes economically heterogeneous.[5] As a result, economic interests among members of the ethnic group would vary tremendously and would take precedence over ethnic group interests. Nathan Glazer's and Daniel Moynihan's work showed that ethnic groups in New York city continue to have importance as "interest groups" and refocused attention on the political consequences of ethnicity.[6] This paper examines the conditions supporting the persistence of ethnicity in politics, using redistricting as an example.

Redistricting: Asian Americans

After each decennial census, the state political districts (assembly, senate, and congressional) are reconfigured to reflect changes in population. Redistricting is critical for ethnic politics because it creates state and federal districts from which officials are elected. Historically, politicians have divided geographic concentrations of ethnic groups into many districts diluting their political influence.

Organizing along ethnic lines is made possible through legal precedent and federal laws. The Voting Rights Act of 1965 and 1982 amendment prohibit minority vote dilution by fragmenting communities.[7] Recent court cases have established the legal basis for creating electoral districts that preserve the political integrity of ethnic groups by keeping communities intact within districts. One of the most important for the Los Angeles region was the 1990 case of *Garza* v. *County of Los Angeles*, which ruled that Latinos had been consistently divided into separate districts. As a result, the Los Angeles County supervisorial districts were redrawn and a Latina, Gloria Molina, was elected to office in the newly created district where Latinos became the majority population group. Oral and written testimony submitted by Asian Americans to the state senate and assembly committees on redistricting focused on these laws and court rulings, stressing the need to keep Asian American communities whole within a district, rather than fragmented in a number of districts.

In their oral and written testimonies submitted to the state assembly and senate committees on redistricting, the Coalition of Asian Pacific Americans for Fair Reapportionment outlined the issues that followed ethnic lines and established the fact that there was such an entity as an "Asian American" community. Anti-Asian American activities, such as hate crimes and English-Only movements, employment discrimination, lack of social service funding, immigration policy, discriminatory admission policies of California state universities, and racist rhetoric by politicians linking immigration to social problems were some of the issues mentioned in the testimony.

Judy Chu, former mayor of Monterey Park and a current member of the city council, addressed some of these issues in her testimony before the Senate committee on elections and reapportionment:

> Without concentrated districts, the ability for Asian Americans to express their concerns about issues will be diluted. For instance, Monterey Park faced an anti-immigrant movement in the mid to late

1980s. There were attempts to restrict languages other than English from being spoken in public, from being written on city materials that went to the public, and from being on commercial signs. There were attempts to prevent foreign-language books from being in our library. While these efforts have been defeated in Monterey Park, some of the issues are still being pushed in other parts of the San Gabriel Valley where there is no organized opposition. . . . Asians need advocates for programs that will help Asian immigrant children and adults learn the English language and make the transition to American society successfully. Unfortunately, those programs are sparse or have long waiting lists.[8]

Leland Saito, in testimony submitted to the assembly committee, cited employment discrimination in Alhambra, the city that borders Monterey Park to the north:

In 1990, the United States Justice Department sued the city of Alhambra and its Fire and Police Departments with charges of employment discrimination against minorities. The U.S. Justice Department does not sue a city unless there is strong evidence of discrimination in hiring and employment procedures and an egregious disparity between the ethnic makeup of the department and surrounding region.[9]

Redistricting was a key issue for Asian Americans, given that no Asian American had been elected to the state legislature in over a decade. The basis for any claim starts with the raw numbers of population and the 127 percent increase of California's Asian American population over the last decade due primarily to immigration. The increase during the past ten years of the Asian American population in cities in the San Gabriel Valley was dramatic. Monterey Park's Asian American population increased by 90.6 percent, bringing the Asian American population to 57.5 percent of the city's population. Similarly, in the nearby cities of Alhambra, Rosemead, and San Gabriel, the Asian American population increased between 289 to 372 percent, forming between 32 to 38 percent of the population in those cities.[10]

The statewide Coalition of Asian Pacific Americans for Fair Reapportionment was formed in 1990 to advocate the interests of Asian Americans and Pacific Islanders to the state legislature which is in charge of the redistricting and reapportionment process.

The Southern California part of the coalition targeted three areas in Los Angeles County with large and rapidly growing Asian American and Pacific Islander populations. They were the Central Los Angeles, South Bay, and San Gabriel Valley areas. Regional coalitions were organized and the San Gabriel Valley Asian Pacific Americans for Fair Reapportionment was established.

The goals included reversing the fragmentation of Asian American and Pacific Islander communities into separate political districts, educating the community about the politics of redistricting and reapportionment, and establishing working ties between ethnic groups in the Asian American and Pacific Islander community as well as with Latinos and African Americans.

Judy Chu, speaking on behalf of the San Gabriel Valley coalition about the fragmentation of the community in testimony to the Senate Committee on Reapportionment, stated:

> Our votes are fractionalized. The cities (in the west San Gabriel Valley). . .are divided into two supervisorial districts, three assembly districts, three senatorial districts, and three congressional districts. It is no wonder that Asians in California are virtually unrepresented anywhere beyond the local level.[11]

Reflecting the demographic mix of the area, most of the members of the San Gabriel Valley group were Chinese American, along with some Japanese American. Republicans and Democrats were active in the non-partisan organization.[12]

The statewide and regional coalitions established themselves before the state legislature as the voices of the Asian American and Pacific Islander community in the redistricting process. However, over time the agenda appeared to be controlled primarily by the native-born and established immigrants, while the more recent immigrants supplied their numbers to give the coalitions legitimacy as representatives of the different communities. Experience with politics, networks with political activists in the different ethnic communities, technical skills needed for the analysis of data, and the knowledge required to testify at government hearings were resources that existed largely among certain members of the community. Employees of social service agencies, college students and professors, staff workers of elected officials, and attorneys were the primary participants in the coalitions.

As a result, negotiations between Asian Americans and Latinos were carried out by a small group of highly-educated professionals who were acutely aware of the need for coalitions because of the tremendous amount of work and resources required to counter the history of gerrymandering that fragmented ethnic communities.

Asian Americans and Latinos

There were major problems to overcome in the development of an alliance between the two ethnic groups. Asian Americans were well aware of the large numbers of Latinos in the San Gabriel Valley and of the fact that Latinos held all county, state, and federal elected offices that included Monterey Park. The needs of Asian Americans could easily be lost in an alliance.

Latinos were concerned about the rapidly growing number of Asian Americans and the threat this posed to growing Latino political power. In fact, when the Southwest Voter Registration and Education Project, a Latino organization, held one of the first voter registration drives in the area for Asian Americans, some Latinos in the region complained about it, saying that resources should be used only for Latinos.[13]

However, despite their differences, several factors encouraged the development of an alliance. Each group recognized the strengths of the other. As newcomers to the process, Asian Americans involved in redistricting were well aware of the need to work with the more experienced Latinos. Asian Americans had much to learn from Latino organizations that had gained political and legal knowledge through their successful court cases, such as *Garza* v. *County of Los Angeles*. Latinos also had the support of organizations with much larger budgets, such as the Mexican American Legal Defence and Education Fund and the Southwest Voter Registration and Education Project. Even though the Asian American population is growing rapidly in the San Gabriel Valley, Latinos are still the largest population group in the area. Also, there were Latino members in the state legislature who would be open to listening to the Latino coalition.

During the first meeting between the two statewide groups in May 1991, an Asian American stated that we were new to the game and looked to Latinos for guidance:

> Asians and Pacific Islanders are at an early stage. We look to the Latino community for help. We want to nurture the relationship, I am encouraged by the sensitivity expressed at this table. We would appreciate your guidance, steps we should take, direction to go in; it's a new process for many of us. Someone later added that we (Asian Americans) are where the Latinos were in the 1960s or 70s.[14]

Latinos were well aware of the tremendous growth of the Asian American population in the valley documented by the 1990 census. Latinos were also aware that this growth was translating into a political force represented by recent successful campaigns to elect Asian Americans to local city councils and school boards. Also, as the late Jesse Unruh reportedly said, "money is the mother's milk of politics" and Asian Americans had a strong record of donating money. Don Nakanishi writes that Asian Americans have become "a major new source of campaign funds, a veritable mountain of gold."[15] In fact, Nakanishi notes that Asian Americans "In the 1988 presidential election. . .were second only to the American Jewish population in the amount of campaign money raised by an ethnic or minority group."[16] The fact that this money could also flow to Latino candidates had already been proven in past campaigns when Asian Americans held fund raisers for state Senator Art Torres in his bid for Los Angeles County Supervisor in the newly created San Gabriel Valley district and for Xavier Becerra and his campaign for the Assembly in 1990.

Although they are the majority of the population, Latinos and Asian Americans still lack representatives in elected offices. For example, in 1991, the city council of Rosemead was all Anglo, despite the fact that Asian Americans and Latinos combined were over 80 percent of the population. In August 1991, during one of the Latino and Asian American meetings to discuss plans, one Latino began to talk about the necessity of building links between Latinos and Asian Americans at all levels.

> We have to work together. In local neighborhoods, cities, the region.
> Working together, Asians and Latinos can offset the disproportionate
> amount of political power held by Anglos. We can work together on
> a project, or elections. The perception among Latinos is that Asians
> have a lot of money, are organized. The newspapers have given this
> a lot of coverage. I have all the articles since this began. We can pool
> our resources, Asians have money and we have numbers.[17]

Asian Americans responded by saying that they were committed to working together because of common issues. Realistically, political realities dictated that Asian Americans must work with Latinos. In fact, Asian Americans already had a long history of working with Latinos and they listed a number of examples.

> I can say that Asians are committed to working with Latinos because
> the political reality is that Asians need Latinos more than Latinos need
> Asians because our population is smaller and we have a low number
> of registered voters. We know we need Latino support to win. In
> fact, we have already started making links. Tomorrow, the local
> Asian Pacific Democratic Club, many of the members of the coalition
> are part of that, are meeting with the San Gabriel Valley LULAC to
> discuss redistricting. The Asian Democratic club walked for Xavier
> Becerra's campaign. Asians volunteered for Art Torres during his
> last campaign. One of the Latinos replied that this was true, he had
> worked on Becerra's campaign and was impressed by the Asian
> turnout.[18]

Asian Americans and Latinos understood that the political clout of both groups supporting one set of redistricting plans for the region would increase the possibility of the legislature adopting the plan. Most important, they also knew that if Asian Americans and Latinos were pitted against one another, both groups could end up losing.

In conclusion, Latinos and Asian Americans recognized that each group could benefit through combined efforts. The enemy was the political establishment and its history of political gerrymandering which fragmented each community, diluting political power and leaving them with leaders who did not have to respond to issues of the Asian American and Latino communities.

Building a State Assembly District

The main concern of the Asian American group was keeping their population together and getting as many Asian Americans as possible into an assembly district. The group checked the 1990 census data and picked out the cities with the largest numbers of Asian Americans. Using this rough guide, the group drew a line around Monterey Park, Alhambra, Rosemead, San Gabriel, South Pasadena, San Marino, and Temple City. To achieve the required amount of about 370,000 people for an assembly district, the group experimented with portions of cities to the north, such as Arcadia, and cities to the east and south, such as El Monte, and Montebello. The group ended up with districts where the Asian American population ranged around 35 percent.

Checking political parties, the districts varied from slightly more Democratic to slightly more Republican. The major difference was going north and east into cities like Arcadia which included more Anglo Republicans while going south brought in more Latino Democrats.

What really interested the group was the voting record in the 1990 California secretary of state election. Flores, an Anglo Republican, was a Los Angeles City Council person for the southern area and little known in the San Gabriel Valley. It is possible that Latinos may have thought that she was Latina because of her last name, acquired through marriage. Checking the data, in the Republican northern cities such as San Marino, Flores won by a wide margin whereas in the Democratic Latino cities, Eu won by a wide margin. The group thought that this was interesting because even though Flores had a Latino last name, incumbency and political party seemed to be more important to the Latino vote. The group was concerned about the northern cities. What did it mean when a very popular moderate Asian American Democrat could not win? After all, Eu had won some past elections with the highest vote totals of anyone running for a statewide office.

Examining the areas of population concentration and growth collided with several political realities. First, creating a district that would maximize Asian American political influence does not necessarily result from just grouping the largest number of Asian Americans possible in one district. The northern cities were areas of heavy Asian American growth but also contained large numbers of politically conservative Anglos who may not support issues important to Asian Americans, such as more open immigration policies and bilingual voting materials. Discussion during a meeting of the Asian American coalition brought out these points as members expressed their concern:

> Some residents in the northern cities were very conservative and the John Birch Society was active there. Another person added, it goes beyond political partisanship because the anti-Asian activity in the north was scary. A recent newspaper article in the *Los Angeles Times* listed a number of incidents, including cross-burnings on lawns of Asian homes. What will inclusion of these areas mean for Asian political interests? Will our interest be served best by someone responding to the interests of conservative Anglos or moderate to liberal Latinos? If a moderate Democrat like March can't win (in the northern cities), what chance does another Asian have? Maybe even an Asian Republican with a strong record with the party may not have a chance.[19]

As one Latino mentioned:

> If the cities with high Asian concentrations were put in one district, would we be creating a district which will not be an Asian influence district? It could possibly be a district where the Asian population would be high, but Anglo registered voters may be the dominant group. If that is so, then an Asian or Latino influence district would be lost in the area.[20]

Second, there was difficulty in reconciling the political rights of the Asian American population, which was under the protection of the Voting Rights Act, and the Latino assemblyman, who as a minority elected official, also came under the Voting Rights Act. He lived in Monterey Park and had expressed his desire to stay there. How would you create a single district which protected his rights as an ethnic incumbent, and also protected the rights of Asian Americans? Adding cities like South Pasadena and San Marino would be out of the question because along with Asian Americans were high numbers of Anglo Republicans who were not likely to vote for a Latino Democrat. Also, the Asian American group did not want to ignore the concerns of the Latino group and damage efforts to build a coalition.

Also, the possibility of a lower voter turnout in the southern cities as compared to the northern cities may favor an Asian American candidate.

> If we go north, we get Republican, high propensity voters, people who may not vote for an Asian. Going south or east, we get Latinos, Democrats. They may not vote for an Asian either, but even in areas

like Montebello which are considered middle-class Latino strongholds, their voting frequency may be less than in northern areas. Because their voter turnout is less, it may be better to go south than north.[21]

The group studied the current 59th district and discussed ways to modify it. Adding Rosemead and San Gabriel would keep the core Asian American population together. The four cities (along with Monterey Park and Alhambra) with the largest and fastest growing Asian American populations would be together. At the same time, by going south, a Latino majority population would be maintained. Solidly Democratic, the area did support March Fong Eu.

With these proposals in mind, the Asian American and Latino groups got together to work out a final plan. One Latino said that they were working hard to develop a plan that considered the concerns of the Asian American community. Therefore they moved Rosemead from the 60th to the plans for the 59th Assembly district. The Latinos agreed that because of its large (34.3 percent) and rapidly growing (371 percent over the past decade) Asian American population, it should go along with Monterey Park. This would also benefit Latinos because it would weaken the Anglo incumbent (assembly district) by taking away a city where she received many of her votes.[22] The strength of the Anglo vote in the city was clear since all the city council members at that time were Anglo.

Adding San Gabriel was tougher for the Latino group. Not currently in the 59th Assembly district, it would add yet another city to Xavier Becerra's Latino district, an additional burden for his reelection campaign. Although there was a solid middle-class community of Latino voters, there was also a large number of high propensity Republican Anglo voters.

Ultimately, adding the four cities of Asian American concentration and growth to the 59th district could be done while still maintaining a district where Latinos and Democrats were well over 50 percent of the population, giving the Latino incumbent a strong base to run on if he decided to seek reelection.

On August 30, 1991, the San Gabriel Valley Latino and Asian American groups, along with representatives from both statewide organizations, held a press conference in Monterey Park's city hall to announce that they had reached agreement on plans for districts in their region. In September, a group of Latinos and Asian Americans went together to Sacramento and met with a number of elected officials to lobby for their joint plan.

The Governor of California, Pete Wilson, vetoed the plans submitted by the state legislature. The state Supreme Court took over the redistricting task and appointed a "special masters" committee to create a new plan. The San Gabriel Valley Asian American and Latino groups coordinated their testimonies to support one another when they spoke before the masters committee.

The state Supreme Court adopted the new plan on January 27, 1992. The plan created a new assembly district, 49, which followed the recommendations of the valley coalition by grouping the four cities of Asian American concentration. The San Gabriel Valley was the only region in the state where such close working ties existed between Asian Americans and Latinos.

Conclusion

Perhaps one of the reasons why Asian Americans and Latinos were able to reach agreement over plans was the demographic balance of the San Gabriel Valley. Clearly, although the Asian American population was rapidly growing, their numbers in terms of registered voters were too small to be a threat to a strong Latino candidate. Therefore, Latinos could agree to the Asian American plan of grouping four cities together without endangering the reelection chances of the incumbent Latino assemblyman. As the Asian American population continued to grow and gain political power, changing the balance of power in the region, forging an alliance could prove to be a much more difficult task.

Asian Americans understood that they were newcomers to the redistricting process and that they would benefit from an alliance with Latinos who had the experience of winning major battles in court which established political rights, had powerful organizations backing their efforts, held all major political offices in the region, and had the largest ethnic population in the state to give them a strong foundation for their claims. In the year 2000, when the next census is taken and the redistricting process occurs again, Asian Americans will no longer be newcomers to the process. The question is, will Asian Americans find it necessary to form a coalition with Latinos? Uniting two groups proved to be much easier when a common enemy existed, the state legislature, which was interested in pitting the two groups against one another. Judging from the experience of the 1990s and the fragmentation of many Asian American and Latino communities throughout the state in the final redistricting plans, the common goal of protecting the political rights of their respective communities could again prove to be a powerful inducement for forming a coalition.

Latinos and Asian Americans also have similar concerns which should continue to provide a basis for a coalition. With large numbers of immigrants in both groups, some of the issues they share include bilingual voting materials, English language classes, and immigration policy. As ethnic groups, they both face employment discrimination as

65

shown in cases filed against the city of Alhambra. Although Latinos had made some headway in terms of electing officials, both groups were faced with politicians who were unresponsive to their concerns.

Unlike the conditions in Los Angeles that sparked the events following the Rodney King decision, such as class divisions following ethnic lines, an educational system in crisis, high unemployment, few services, and deteriorating housing stock, the San Gabriel Valley had a significant middle class population. Also, there were a number of Latino and Asian American individuals and organizations in existence that had a history of working together.[23] The difficult task of building working relations was made easier because of such existing ties. Politically experienced and economically stable, the residents were able to get involved with what is for the average person, an abstract political concept that seemed to have little to do with the reality of their day-to-day lives.

In contrast to the San Gabriel Valley coalitions around a set of plans, the Los Angeles downtown Asian American and Latino groups basically agreed to disagree and not attack one another. Major differences between Los Angeles and the San Gabriel Valley might explain why agreement was reached in one place but not the other. First, the Asian American population mix in downtown was much more complex, with well developed Japanese, Chinese, Korean, and Filipino communities as compared to the San Gabriel Valley which was dominated by Chinese and Japanese Americans.[24] Organizing the individual Asian American communities and then meeting together as a unified group was a more complicated and lengthy process.[25] In addition, the San Gabriel Valley Asian American population was more experienced politically because of its longer history of working on the campaigns of local Asian American candidates. Networks and organizations were already in place which could begin work on redistricting.

Second, the downtown Asian American and Latino populations were spread out over a much larger area, with miles separating some of the communities as compared to the four contiguous cities in the San Gabriel Valley Asian American plan. Third, the overall demographic mix of the downtown area was more complicated with a large population of African Americans who were nearly absent (about 1 percent) in the San Gabriel Valley. This required taking into consideration the political rights of another group, making the process much more complex. Fourth, downtown Los Angeles contained some of the most expensive real estate in the state, making it the site of much larger political battles than in the San Gabriel Valley. As a result of these four factors, Los Angeles presented a more complex set of circumstances that had to be worked out among more participants.

In summary, organizing along ethnic lines was made possible by federal law and legal precedent which established the political rights of communities as defined by ethnicity. Understanding the political nature of redistricting, Asian Americans and Latinos put aside their differences and combined their resources to fight the common enemy, the political establishment and its history of political gerrymandering, which had fragmented Asian American and Latino communities for so long.

Notes

This research was supported in part by a Rockefeller Foundation Fellowship in the Humanities administered by the UCLA Asian American Studies Center and an American Sociological Asociation Minority Fellowship funded by the National Institute on Mental Health.

1. Paul M. Ong, *Asian Pacific Islanders in California, 1990* (Los Angeles: Asian American Studies Center, University of California, Los Angeles, 1991).

2. Illsoo Kim, *New Urban Immigrants: The Korean Community in New York* (Princeton, New Jersey: Princeton University Press, 1981); Peter Kwong, *The New Chinatown* (New York: Hill and Wang, 1987); S. Frank Miyamoto, *Social Solidarity among the Japanese in Seattle* (Seattle, Washington: University of Washington Press, 1984); Victor G. Nee, and Brett de Bary Nee, *Longtime Californ': A Documentary Study of an American Chinatown* (Stanford: Stanford University Press, 1986).

3. Edward Chang, "New Urban Crisis: Korean-Black Conflict in Los Angeles" (Ph.D. Dissertation, University of California at Berkeley, 1990); Melvin L. Oliver and James H. Johnson, "Inter-Ethnic Conflict in an Urban Ghetto: The Case of Blacks and Latinos in Los Angeles," *Research in Social Movements, Conflict and Change* 6 (1984):57-94.

4. Milton M. Gordon, *Assimilation in American Life* (New York: Oxford University Press, 1964):27.

5. Robert A. Dahl, *Who Governs? Democracy and Power in an American City* (New Haven, Connecticut: Yale University Press, 1973).

6. Nathan Glazer and Daniel P. Moynihan, *Beyond the Melting Pot* (Cambridge, Massachusetts: MIT Press, 1986):17.

7. Chandler Davidson, editor, *Minority Vote Dilution* (Washington D.C.: Howard University Press, 1984).

8. Judy Chu, March 9, 1991. Testimony delivered in Los Angeles to the California Senate Committee on Elections and Reapportionment.

9. Leland Saito, June 28, 1991. Testimony delivered in Los Angeles to the California Assembly Committee on Elections, Reapportionment and Constitutional Amendments.

10. Ong.

11. Chu, March 9, 1991.

12. Don Nakanishi, "The Next Swing Vote? Asian Pacific Americans and California Politics" in Byran O. Jackson and Michael B. Preston, eds. *Racial and Ethnic Politics in California* (Berkeley: IGS Press, 1991).

13. Jose Z. Calderon, "Mexican American Politics in a Multi-Ethnic Community: The Case of Monterey Park: 1985-1990." Ph.D. dissertation, UCLA, 1991.

14. Statement of a member of the Los Angeles Asian American Coalition during a meeting in Los Angeles on May 24, 1991.

15. Nakanishi, 47.

16. Nakanishi, 47.

17. Statement of a member of the San Gabriel Valley Latino Coalition during a meeting between the Valley groups on August 8, 1991.

18. Statement of a member of the San Gabriel Valley Asian American Coalition during a meeting between Valley groups on August 8, 1991.

19. Discussion during a San Gabriel Valley Asian American Coalition meeting on July 30, 1991.

20. A member of the Latino California state coalition during a meeting with the California state Asian American coalition on June 26, 1991, in Los Angeles.

21. A member of the San Gabriel Valley Asian American coalition during a meeting on June 27, 1992.

22. Discussion during meeting between the Asian American and Latino San Gabriel Valley coalitions on August 8, 1991.

23. Leland T. Saito, "Politics in a New Demographic Era: Asian Americans in Monterey Park, California." Ph.D. dissertation, UCLA, 1992.

24. _____, "Japanese Americans and the New Chinese Immigrants: The Politics of Adaptation," *California Sociologist* 12 (1989):195-211. Leland T. Saito and John Horton, "The Chinese Immigration and the Rise of Asian American Politics in Monterey Park, California" in Edna Bonacich, Paul Ong, and Lucie Cheng, eds. *Struggles for a Place: The New Asian Immigration in the Restructuring Political Economy* (Philadelphia: Temple University Press, 1993).

25. Yen Le Espiritu, *Asian American Panethnicity: Bridging Institutions and Identities* (Philadelphia: Temple University Press, 1992).

The South Central Los Angeles Eruption:
A Latino Perspective

Armando Navarro

On April 29, 1992, the city of Los Angeles erupted like an angry volcano with all the fury of a lava stream of frustration and anger. The unprecedented convulsion of violence, destruction, and death has been described by writers as a riot, rebellion, disorder, disturbance, and uprising. However described, it awoke the nation to the painful reality of the precarious deteriorating condition of race relations in most American cities. The eruption was precipitated by the "not guilty" verdict rendered in the trial of the four Los Angeles police officers charged with unlawfully beating African American Rodney King. The verdict created a contagion of disorder, looting, and killing that continued from April 29 to May 2 and was unmatched in its destructiveness in American history.

Though the media initially portrayed the "eruption of discontent" as one involving primarily African Americans and Koreans, the reality was that it was the first multiethnic eruption in the nation's history. In particular, Latinos became both protagonists and victims of the explosion consequently becoming major participants in what this author describes as the explosion of discontent. This article provides an analysis of the changing demographics of South Central Los Angeles; the Latino role in the eruption; the etiology of the eruption; the rift the eruption created among the various ethnic and racial groups; and analysis of the eruption from a policy perspective.

ARMANDO NAVARRO is an assistant professor in the Department of Ethnic Studies at the University of California at Riverside.

South Central Los Angeles:
Latinos, the New Ethnic Majority

In order to understand the Latino role in the eruption and its aftermath, we must examine the changing demographics of South Central Los Angeles (SCLA).[1] In the past decade, Latino immigrants from Mexico and Central America, particularly from El Salvador and Guatemala,

	Study Area	Los Angeles City	Los Angeles County
Table 1			
1980 Census: Racial and Ethnic Changes in Los Angeles			
Total Population	2,481,583	2,968,036	7,477,503
White	788,078 31.8%	1,420,476 47.9%	3,953,603 52.9%
African American	729,449 29.4%	505,199 17.0%	943,968 12.6%
Latino	772,160 31.1%	816,170 27.5%	2,066,103 27.6%
Blacks of Hispanic Origin	12,352 1.6%	9,487 1.2%	17,608 0.9%
Asian & Pacific Islander	172,741 7.0%	196,044 6.6%	434,850 5.8%
Chinese	35,389 1.4%	44,362 1.5%	93,747 1.3%
Japanese	51,690 2.1%	49,345 1.7%	116,543 1.6%
Korean	28,011 1.1%	33,066 1.1%	60,618 0.8%
Filipino	34,606 1.4%	43,718 1.5%	99,043 1.3%

have moved into the area formerly perceived as dominated by African Americans. In 1990, approximately 46 percent of the residents of SCLA were Latinos, making them the largest ethnic group.[2] This demographic transformation can be understood by making a comparative analysis of the 1980 and 1990 census.

In the 1980 census, Latinos in the SCLA comprised approximately only 31 percent of the population. At that time, Latinos, Whites, and African Americans were almost identical in population numbers. The following table illustrates this point[3]:

Table 2

1990 Census: Racial and Ethnic Changes in Los Angeles

	Study Area	Los Angeles City	Los Angeles County
Total	2,784,125	3,485,398	8,863,164
White	609,349 21.9%	1,302,023 37.4%	3,618,850 40.8%
African American	682,331 24.5%	487,674 13.9%	1,941,552 21.9%
Latino	1,280,220 46.0%	1,391,411 39.9%	3,351,242 37.8%
Blacks of Hispanic Origin	39,969 9.1%	33,385 1.0%	58,198 0.7%
Chinese	46,460 1.7%	67,196 1.9%	245,033 2.8%
Japanese	44,165 1.6%	45,370 1.3%	129,736 1.5%
Korean	57,644 2.1%	72,970 2.1%	145,431 1.6%
Filipino	56,001 2.0%	87,625 2.5%	219,653 2.5%

By 1990, the Latino population had increased substantially while the African American and white populations had declined, with a slight increase for Asian Americans. Table 2 illustrates these changes:[4]

The demographic statistics of SCLA suggest that what was once perceived as primarily an African American area is becoming an ocean of Latino humanity. This transformation is a product of an influx of hundreds of thousands of economic and political refugees from both Central America and Mexico. During the 1980s, these refugees, fleeing from the horrors of political upheaval and revolution in Central America and a concomitant economic crisis in Mexico, found a haven in the midst of the SCLA. Consequently, by the year 2000 Latinos will compose the indisputable majority ethnic group of SCLA. By way of illustration, Latinos in 1990 outnumbered African Americans in Watts and constituted 46 percent of the Watts population. Even in Koreatown, Latinos outnumbered Koreans. They comprised 48 percent of the population to the Koreans' 3 percent.[5] Thus SCLA's changing demographics was a critical factor in analyzing the Latino role both during and after the eruption.

Latinos and the SCLA Eruption

When the "not guilty" verdicts were rendered that afternoon on April 29, what began as a political protest at Parker Center, the headquarters of the Los Angeles Police Department, spread like a wildfire of anger and engulfed entire sections of SCLA. This eruption soon became socially targeted and other violence took the form of arson and looting. A summary report produced by the Tomas Rivera Center entitled "Latinos and the Uprising: The Economic Context," stated that "both the verdict and the subsequent social disorder dismayed and challenged a city that had long boasted of its multicultural and internationalist future."[6]

Because the mass media giants portrayed the eruption as primarily one of African American and Asian American violence, and because of a relative absence of disorder in the East Los Angeles Latino community, the general impression was that Latinos were only involved peripherally in the events of April 29–May 2. *Los Angeles Times* staff writers George Ramos and Tracy Wilkinson wrote:

> Though largely portrayed in the national media as a Black uprising, the riots in fact involved many Latinos, both as victims and vandals. One third of those killed and at least as many arrested for looting and other crimes were Latino; Latino-owned businesses were destroyed and many Latinos were left homeless by arson.[7]

The slant of the media was obvious. The front page of *Newsweek* pictured a young African American in front of a burning building.[8] *Time* magazine did likewise.[9] However, as the eruption progressed, the media began to acknowledge the ethnic diversity of those participating in the melee.

Looting and arson occurred in Latino and Asian American as well as African American neighborhoods and even reached into white districts in Venice, Beverly Hills, and the San Fernando Valley. The original three flash points of the eruption occurred in Hyde Park, where Latinos constituted 26 percent of the population, at the intersection of Florence and Normandie where Latinos comprised 28 percent, and at the intersection of Martin Luther King, Jr. Boulevard and Normandie, where Latinos made up 54 percent of the population.[10] Joan Petersilia, the RAND Corporation criminologist who conducted a study on the eruption acknowledged that "this was clearly not a Black riot. It was a minority riot."[11]

Furthermore, according to Rose Institute's SCLA Atlas, "of the first 23 acts of violence reported by emergency calls to the Los Angeles Police Department between 3:00 P.M. and 7:00 P.M. on April 29, eight occurred in neighborhoods where Latinos constituted a majority of the population.[12] Moreover, 51 percent of those arrested were Latino; 30 percent of those who died were Latino; and up to 40 percent of the damaged businesses were Latino-owned."[13] The Los Angeles Police Department reported that of the 5,438 arrested from April 30 to Monday morning of May 4, 1993, 2,764 were Latino, 2,022 African American, 568 white, and 84 classified as other. In addition, 19 of the 58 people killed in the eruption were Latino and the most damaged neighborhoods were Latino.[14]

Adding to the unprecedented nature of the eruption was the direct participation of Latino immigrants. According to the Immigration and Naturalization Service (INS) officials, undocumented immigrants accounted for more than 1,200 of the 15,000 people arrested. The *Los Angeles Times* reported that on one occasion of 477 undocumented immigrants picked up and handed over to the INS, 360 were from Mexico, 62 from El Salvador, 35 from Guatemala, 14 from Honduras, 2 from Jamaica, and the rest from other countries.[15] During the three days of looting, arson and violence, the Los Angeles Police Department conducted sweeps throughout the various barrios of SCLA. The Los Angeles police officers disregarded the long-standing policy of not being pro-active in apprehending undocumented immigrants and turning them over to the INS for probable deportation. The Mexican, Salvadoran, Guatemalan, and Honduran Consulates asked Mayor Tom Bradley to "respect immigrants' human rights" regardless of their migrant status.[16] Thus, Latinos from such sub-groups joined in the violence giving the riot a multiethnic coloring.

The Etiology of the Eruption

An abundance of literature in the social sciences exists on the etiology of violence. Scholars have propounded numerous theories, paradigms, and ideas, all seeking to shed some light on the causation of violence. Using a Marxist framework, some economists and sociologists accentuate the inevitability of class struggle, meaning that the antagonisms and contradictions of a capitalist society produce increasing misery and ultimately a convulsion of violence directed by the proletariat against the ruling bourgeoisie. Political scientists and psychologists such as Ted Gurr, James Davies, and others stress some form of relative deprivation.[17] Other social scientists contend that violent eruptions such as that in SCLA stem from structural deficiencies within the system.[18]

The SCLA explosion, in my view, can be better understood etiologically within the context of relative deprivation (RD). Essentially, RD is predicated on frustration-aggression theory. In its most basic sense, RD refers to the gap between what people have and what they think they should have. As Gurr wrote about RD, it is a "perceived discrepancy between people's value expectations and their value capabilities." Specifically, value expectations are the goods and conditions of life to which people believe they are rightfully entitled, whereas value capabilities are the goods and conditions that they think they are capable of attaining or maintaining. Frustration, discontent, and ultimately aggressive are the by-products of discrepancy between expectations and capabilities and determine the scope and intensity of RD.[19] In essence, RD fosters popular discontent and frustration which in turn intensifies to the point of engendering a climate of discontent.

Yet the pervasiveness of dissatisfaction is not alone sufficient to foster violence. As social scientists Chalmers Johnson, Harry Eckstein and others have written, it takes some event, person, incident, etc. to precipitate the violence. To Johnson it was an "accelerator" and to Eckstein it was a "precipitant." The "accelerators" or "precipitant" are the final or immediate causes of revolutionary violence. They are discrete events such as military defeat, economic crisis, governmental violence, reforms, and so forth, that occur at a specific point in time.[20] A precipitant, according to Eckstein, is an event which actually starts the revolutionary violence, "much as turning the flintwheel of a cigarette lighter ignites the flame."[21] Thus, RD coupled with an accelerator or precipitant provides this analysis with a conceptual framework that is useful in explaining the etiology of the SCLA eruption.

This climate of discontent was the product of a major discrepancy between the people's value expectations and value capabilities. This applied to all of the diverse ethnic groups that participated in the mayhem. For Latinos, their value expectations exceeded their value capabilities. Many Latinos of SCLA are immigrants from Mexico, El Salvador, Guatemala, Honduras, and other parts of Latin America. They came to the United States motivated by rising expectations for a better quality of life. Spurred by determination, courage, and hope, they overcame much suffering in their precarious journeys to the United States—only to find themselves once again impacted by the omnipresence of a hostile and impoverished environment. Once settled, they became immersed and consumed by American society's materialist and consumer-oriented values and beliefs. But their impoverished status precluded them from realizing their expectations which in turn produced a growing frustration.

Based on content analysis of numerous reports, newspaper, and magazine articles, coupled with radio and television commentaries, I argue that the SCLA eruption was predictable and even inevitable considering the impoverished socioeconomic components and deteriorating race relations of the area. The SCLA is comprised of economically impoverished enclaves that are plagued by high unemployment and underemployment, crime, gang violence, drug and alcohol abuse, dilapidated housing, high educational dropout rates, etc. In other words, SCLA was an extremely fertile ground for an urban upheaval. It had a whirlwind climate of discontent that was breeding popular frustration and anger.

The pervasiveness of poverty therefore was a precondition to the eruption. The Tomas Rivera Study purports that the difficult economic conditions affecting SCLA led to the eruption. Particularly for Latinos, poverty in SCLA has been increasing. In Los Angeles, the percentage of Latino families falling below the poverty line was three times higher than that of non-Latino families. The study further stated that in 1989 Latino per capita income in Los Angeles was $7,111, less than half the city's average. Of Latinos living in SCLA, it was much lower, $4,461, which translates to 63 percent of the area's already low level.[22] Eden Porter, author of the Tomas Rivera report, corroborates this author's contention when he said, "This was a bread riot. . . . This uprising was a response to economic frustration."[23] The precipitant, or accelerator, that ignited the fire was the "not guilty" verdict.

The foregoing income indicators speak for the omnipresence of poverty and the underclass status of many Latino residents of SCLA. Both the Tomas Rivera and Rose Institute research concluded that SCLA is characterized by high unemployment and higher rates of female heads of household. Economic deprivation is further exacerbated by the lack of affordable and decent housing; the pervasiveness of gang violence; drug and alcohol abuse; high crime rates; and lack of political representation, participation and alienation—all of which have added to the status of the Latino underclass. While Latinos encompass over 46 percent of SCLA population, they make up only 5 percent of the registered voters.[24]

Latinos of SCLA perceived themselves as isolated and powerless to do anything about their plight. A survey conducted by Bendixen and Associates and commissioned by KVEA-TV, channel 52, and *La Opinión* newspaper in April 1993, concluded that most Latinos and African Americans in SCLA think that the Los Angeles political leadership cares little about neighborhood problems and has done little to ease racial conflict. When asked, "How much do you feel Los Angeles government and political leaders care about the problems of your neighborhood?" 82 percent responded, "only a little" or "not at all." The response, "a great deal" received a mere 11 percent.[25] Morrie Goldman, spokesperson for Councilman Mike Hernandez, said about the survey, "the problems were created before we came there. We're going in and fixing what City Hall had created over the years."[26]

It is not difficult to understand the results of the preceding survey if one examines the weak and mixed response of Latino elected officials toward the L.A. riots. Most Latino officials from the Los Angeles area were quick to congratulate their Eastside constituency for restraint shown during the eruption. After all, very little looting occurred east of the Los Angeles River. On May 8, 1992, the *Los Angeles Times* reported that Latino elected officials, with the exception of Councilman Mike Hernandez, distanced themselves from the violence. "They appeared. . .eager to distance themselves from what some officials called the less stable Latino enclaves of Pico-Union and South Los Angeles, which are populated by more recent immigrants and which were caught in the eye of the fire storm."[27] Councilman Richard Alatorre said, "I try my best to be an advocate for immigrant concerns. But I didn't get elected to represent them. I have a responsibility to the people I happen to represent."[28]

The frustration of Latino residents of SCLA toward Latino elected officials was evident in numerous comments made by Latino immigrant organizational spokespersons. Carlos Vaquerano, an official with the Central American Refugee Center, said, "there are many Latino leaders who say they represent Latinos, but they do not represent all Latinos."[29] Madeline Janis, Executive Director of the Center, in imploring Latinos to unite, commented, "There's going to be a big backlash now because immigrants are an easy target, and if we don't have the established Latino leadership defending the rights of the newer immigrants, then we are going to be in an even more desperate situation that we are in."[30]

However, this climate of discontent was also a product of race and ethnic degradation, meaning the existence of racism and prejudice towards people of color by certain segments of white society. This form of degradation has increased and impeded the realization of an improvement in the overall quality of life. In spite of such legislation as the Civil Rights Act (1964) and the Voting Rights Act (1965), the struggle for civil rights and economic justice is far from over. The Rodney King incident coupled with the "not guilty" verdict of the four police officers illustrate the deterioration of race relations. The Kerner Commission Report of 1968 concluded that the United States was moving in the direction of a dual society, one Black and the other White. In the context of 1992, this conclusion is incorrect. The truth is that America is drifting towards a society divided four-fold by color, meaning Whites, Latinos, African Americans, and Asians. *Time* magazine, in its cover story of April 9, 1990 entitled "America's Changing Colors" stated that by the year 2056 people of color will comprise the new majority population—the "browning of America." Much of this phenomenon is attributable to immigration and high fertility rates. This situation has fostered a resurgence of "racism" and "nativism," particularly against Latino immigrants, leading to Latino "immigrant-bashing" by other ethnic and racial groups as well as by the dominant white society. Such bashing has been evident even among this nation's elected officials—both Republican and Democrat—who use the immigrant as a "scapegoat" for this nation's myriad ills. This form of degradation has resulted in the deprivation of opportunity the Latino immigrants of SCLA who are at the bottom of the socio-economic and political ladder. These factors explain why Latinos were both protagonists and victims of the eruption.

Unrest Widens Rift among Ethnic Groups

The aftermath of the eruption witnessed a growing rift among the diverse ethnic and racial groups of SCLA. I have accentuated deprivation predicated on economic, political, and racial factors to explain the eruption, rivalry and antagonism among SCLA ethnic and racial groups prior to, during and after the eruption. Prior to the eruption, antagonisms had risen to volatile levels between African Americans and Korean Americans, Latinos and African Americans, Whites and African Americans. Examples of these conflict situations include: 1) the growing tensions between Korean Americans and African Americans as manifested by the shooting of the African American youth Latasha Harlins by a Korean grocery store owner; 2) the escalating conflict between Latino and African Americans over the issue of affirmative action at the Martin Luther King, Jr., Hospital; and 3) the increasing conflict between whites and

African Americans over the issue of police brutality as exemplified by the Rodney King beating.

The aftermath of the eruption has led to an escalation of tensions between African Americans and Latino leaders. With the nation's economic crisis fostering a scarcity of resources, jobs, and other opportunities, the two communities have been on a collision course for years. According to Antonio Rodriguez and Carlos Chavez, who wrote an editorial article in the *Los Angeles Times* entitled "The Rift Is Exposed: Let's Bridge It,"

> Acrimonious debate has raged over the county's affirmative action program, the reapportionment plans of the city, the county and board of education, the hiring practices at places like Martin Luther King Hospital and the competition for the position of Los Angeles chief, to name a few.[31]

This fostering of tension was exacerbated during the eruption. The number of Latinos killed, businesses looted, and buildings destroyed suggest that even though the looters were of various ethnic groups, the riots served to accelerate the tensions among these groups, especially between Latinos and African Americans. The precipitant or accelerator to the "open conflict" between the two groups was the post-eruption rebuilding efforts under the aegis of Rebuild L. A., led by co-chairman Peter Ueberroth. Rebuild L.A. was established for the purpose of securing millions of dollars of investments from the private sector to rebuilt the shattered areas of SCLA. This entailed convincing corporations to act as catalysts for development. Perceiving opportunities for resources and jobs, the leadership of both communities began openly competing for who was going to control the bigger pieces of the pie.

While noble in its intent, Rebuild L.A. became a political issue between the leadership of both communities. In part this was ascribable to its composition. Joel Kotkin, a contributing editor to *Opinión*, wrote:

> The ruling elites seem determined to recreate the failed pattern of the "broker state" through Rebuild L.A. This is evident in Rebuild's core economic leadership—drawn, with few exceptions, from the remnant of the old Anglo downtown Establishment. At the same time, most minorities on the Rebuild board seem out of the 60's central casting: professional supplicants, social service providers and politicians.[32]

The preceding set the stage for the rhetorical war that ensued between the leadership of both communities. In July 1992, Latino office holders sent Mayor Tom Bradley a letter complaining that Latinos were being excluded from post-eruption rebuilding efforts. Led by Councilman Richard Alatorre and Mike Hernandez, the letter stated:

The changing demographics of the inner city must be recognized. As such, it is only just that both the public and private sectors make every effort to ensure that jobs, funds, and other resources are distributed in a fashion that strives to reach parity with the ethnic composition of the very communities we are attempting to restore.[33]

This letter was a product of the war of words that had already begun between Xavier Hermosillo, chairman of N.E.W.S. of America, and Danny Bakewell from the Brotherhood Crusade, with both writing articles critical of the other in the *Los Angeles Times*.[34]

This verbal contest inevitably spilled over into the communities of SCLA. During the summer months of 1992, Bakewell initiated a highly publicized campaign to close down Los Angeles construction sites that did not employ African Americans. Hermosillo responded by organizing "sting teams" of undercover construction workers with video cameras that monitored work sites that employed Latino workers to record Bakewell's efforts to replace Latino workers with African Americans.[35]

Such incidents continued to occur to the point that in September 1992 Latino business and social leaders orchestrated a large press conference rally at City Hall at which it was alleged that Latinos had been shortchanged. The newly-formed Latino Coalition for a New Los Angeles, including the city's two Latino council persons, called for Mayor Bradley to release a breakdown of the financial aid administered by the city's various departments. The coalition also requested the same from President Bush and the federal government. In addition, the City Hall demonstration called on business and industry leaders to create more job opportunities for Latinos.[36] Coalition spokesperson Fernando Oaxaca acknowledged that part of the problem in the past had been that Latinos had been slow to mobilize in public protest. Joe Sanchez, President of the Mexican American Grocers Association, asserted his conviction that African American organizations had received disproportionate attention and post-eruption aid because they had stronger ties to City Hall and because the news media too often painted the eruption as a Black versus White or Black versus Korean conflict in which Latinos were primarily looters instead of victims.[37]

The fact was that the interethnic rifts of SCLA also involved Latinos and Asian Americans. This meant that the eruption played itself out along ethnic lines.[38] In the Pico-Union as in African American neighborhoods, outsider-owned stores, particularly those owned and run by Korean Americans, were looted and destroyed. Carlos Vaquerano of the Central American Refugee Center, whose officers are located in the Pico-Union area, said, "Some Latinos complain about being treated with a lack of respect by Korean merchants—not all of them, but some." As Ruben

Martinez in his article entitled "This Was about Something to Eat" stated, "Many Latinos use the term *Chino* for Asians regardless of whether they are Japanese, Chinese or Thai, and ethnic jokes abound."[39] The reality is that the eruption proved that Latinos were not immune from the vices of prejudice and bigotry.

A Latino Perspective on the Eruption

The eruption was but the calm before the storm. The frustration and anger that exploded on April 29, 1992, remains. Unless major economic and political changes take place and race and ethnic relations improve, Los Angeles will be subject to further "balkanization" that will continue to pit ethnic and racial groups against each other. If the balkanization continues, it could well create a similar scenario of "ethnic cleansing" such as that occurring in Bosnia-Herzegovina, the former Soviet Union, and other parts of the world. Evidence of this scenario, is a plot unveiled by the Federal Bureau of Investigation on July 15, 1993, of an attempt by "skin heads" to precipitate a race war by assassinating certain African-American and Jewish leaders and the bombing of the First African Methodist Church located in SCLA.[40] This aborted plot by the skin heads also made mention of targeting Latinos, which is indicative of a powerful current of nativism which in 1993 heightened tensions among the nation's diverse populations. Similar hate crimes are becoming increasingly prevalent in other American cities.

The nation and California's economy are plagued by increasing poverty, unemployment, the exodus of industry, and social problems. From the federal to the state to the local level, government is increasingly incapable of fiscally meeting the exigencies of the urban crisis. The inability of these governmental entities to act in bringing about change to areas such as SCLA is heightening the people's level of frustration and discontent. This pervasive economic crisis is fostering conflict and tensions among not only ethnic and racial groups, but among the "have-nots," "have-little-want more," and the "have-it-all-want more" socioeconomic classes. American society today is becoming increasingly class-stratified. This reality is apropos in understanding the socioeconomic make-up of SCLA and other American cities.

The lack of commitment by the federal government is shown by its failure to provide adequate assistance relief via the Federal Emergency Management Agency to victims. According to the *Los Angeles Times*, "denial rates for nearly all Federal grant and loan programs are running at fifty percent or higher, leaving many victims and their advocates with a sense that the aid process is not working."[41] At the local level, even the efforts initiated by Rebuild L. A. were being scaled down in

1993.[42] Jin H. Lee, owner of a Compton store that burned down to the ground, stated "I do not hate the people who burned my store. I hate the government that did not do its job because we are a minority."[43] To date, there is no governmental entity at any level that is designed or equipped to effectively deal with the consequences of the such events as the eruption of SCLA.

Without the federal government stepping in and developing a comprehensive "Urban Marshall Plan" that can produce jobs, improve schools, build adequate housing, clean up crime and drugs, provide health care, and involve the people in the reconstruction of their cities, the eruption of SCLA portends worse crises. It is a race against time that will not be won by the power of politicians and activist rhetoric, but rather, through the intervention of governmental and private sectors and their coming together with the people as partners in the rebuilding of America's decaying cities.

The consequences of the eruption for Latinos are even worse. SCLA is becoming heavily Latino. By the twenty-first century, Latinos will be the largest ethnic group in the city and comprise over 50 percent of its population. Peace in Central America will more than likely slow the exodus of immigrants. However, the exodus from Mexico will continue, regardless of the condition of the Mexican economy. The difference is that if the Mexican economy does not improve, the scope and intensity of the exodus will be greater. This translates to the possibility of Latinos in SCLA being relegated to a quasi-"South African syndrome" status, where Latinos will constitute the majority of the population, yet the non-Latino minority will control the economic and political power. This syndrome manifests itself through the denial of economic opportunities for Latino as exemplified in the case of the Latino street vendors who are being run out of business due to insensitive city bureaucratic politics. The immigrant bashing has intensified to a fever pitch where in California, both Republican and Democrat, federal and state officials have proposed scores of restrictive and racist immigration policies directed at the Latino immigrant. One illustration of this is U.S. Senator Dianne Feinstein's efforts to curb illegal immigration. She said at a Senate Judiciary Committee Hearing held on May 19, 1993, that "It is up to this government and this (Justice) Department to control the border. . . . Unless we deal with it, there is going to be a terrible backlash. . .a long backlash in the future."[44] Concurrently, state legislators have become embroiled in the immigrant bashing by the introduction of twenty-one bills, all aimed at curbing immigration and the denial of services and benefits to the undocumented.[45]

In order to avoid this negative scenario, Latinos must put aside their differences and forge powerful alliances among themselves that are based on popular participation. Politicians need to be held accountable via the power of an organized, politicized, and registered populace. To accomplish this, massive political education efforts must be initiated to convince the thousands of legal immigrants to become naturalized citizens and to vote. The same must be done for the United States native-born Latinos who reside in SCLA.

The most powerful weapon the people have with which to obviate a South African syndrome is the formation of powerful grass-roots organizations led by individuals indigenous to SCLA. These organizations must be supported financially by the people themselves and by the private and public sectors. Latinos in SCLA must work to create an infrastructure similar to the political machines of the past that were able to promote change and opportunity for the immigrant population. Furthermore, with money being the lubricant for change and empowerment, Latinos in SCLA must design economic, political and social developmental plans that will with time empower them and give them control of their own *barrio* economies, political structures, and social institutions. Self-sufficiency and self-reliance in these times of economic crises must guide the actions of these plans.

Concomitantly, if Latinos are to avoid another disruption, they must seek to form coalitions with other ethnic and social groups. Inter-ethnic coalition-building is a must. Latinos must be willing to share economic and political power. Other groups must be willing to do the same. The Latino's growing population has value both politically in the vote and economically in the form of purchasing power. Hence, accords must be reached so that the rifts and conflicts are mitigated and a more united development process is realized that is beneficial to all. As long as ethnic groups are at each other's throats fighting for the meager crumbs of governmental handouts, SCLA as a whole will lose. Every group must realize that other groups are not the enemies; the enemies are the policies of local, state, and federal entities of a society that is in transition from a Cold War to a peace economy.

To date, the nation is plagued by an inability of the capitalist economic system to provide jobs and hope for a better future for the people of America. Without a major change in the policies of the nation's economic system, there is no hope for ethnic majorities who live in places like SCLA. Even if Latinos were to become the political majority on the city council, with a Latino mayor, what difference would it make when elected officials are powerless to act because Los Angeles is financially strapped? Without the resources to provide jobs, social services, viable educational systems, housing, public safety, health, etc., the future of SCLA and other urban areas looks bleak.

Only through the creation of a Latino unified effort will the barrios of SCLA and the rest of Los Angeles be transformed from islands of deprivation to communities of prosperity. Latinos must also participate in the formation of multiethnic/racial coalitions which are predicated on the inclusion of all groups and segments who share a common interest in the rebuilding of SCLA and Los Angeles. However, this will also pose a challenge to all the groups involved, for it means that the coalition must be built on the principal of "power" and "benefit" sharing. All groups must realize that for a community to progress as a whole will require that everyone share in the "power of governing" and "benefits of prosperity".

Notes

1. Any analysis of the eruption of SCLA must take into account the factor of what constitutes SCLA. There is no clear agreement as to what exactly is the geographic make-up of SCLA. The boundary lines selected for SCLA will impact the results of the research—particularly when citing statistics concerning SCLA's racial, ethnic, and socioeconomic characteristics. For purposes of analysis, the author is using the definition of SCLA developed by Claremont McKenna College's Rose Institute of Local and State Government in their book of SCLA entitled *An Atlas of South Central Los Angeles*. Published in 1992 by the Rose Institute, the atlas defines SCLA as "bounded by West Hollywood and Beverly Hills on the Northwest; Culver City, Ladera Heights, Inglewood, Lennox, and Hawthorne on the West; Lawndale, Gardena, and Compton on the South; and Lynwood, South Gate, Huntington Park, and Vernon on the East." Not all of the study area is in Los Angeles. Of the 526 census tracts included, only 346 are in the City of Los Angeles.

2. Stuart Anderson, Adrian Dove, Armando Navarro, Ralph Rossum, Robert S. Walters, et al., *An Atlas of South-Central Los Angeles* (Claremont, California: Rose Institute of Local and State Government, 1992), 8.

3. *Ibid.*

4. *Ibid.*

5. *Ibid.*, 4.

6. *Ibid.*, 1.

7. *Los Angeles Times*, May 8, 1992.

8. *Newsweek*, May 11, 1992.

9. *Time*, May 11, 1992.

10. *An Atlas of South-Central Los Angeles*, 4.

11. *Los Angeles Times*, June 18, 1992.

12. *An Atlas of South-Central Los Angeles*, 4.

13. Manuel Pastor, *Latinos and the Los Angeles Uprising: The Economic Context* (Claremont, California: Tomas Rivera Center, 1993), 1.

14. *Los Angeles Times*, May 11, 1992.

15. *Ibid.*

16. *Ibid.*

17. Ted Robert Gurr, *Why Men Rebel* (Princeton, New Jersey: Princeton Press, 1970); James C. Davies, "The J-Curve of Rising and Declining as a Cause of Some Great Revolutions and a Contained Rebellion," in *The History of Violence in America;* Carl Leiden and Karl Schmitt, *The Politics of Violence: Revolution in the Modern World* (Englewood Cliffs, New Jersey: Prentice-Hall, 1968).

18. Chalmers Johnson, *Revolution and the Social System* (Stanford, California: Stanford University, Hoover Institution, 1964).

19. *Why Men Rebel,* 13.

20. Thomas H. Greene, *Comparative Revolutionary Movements* (Englewood Cliffs, New Jersey: Prentice-Hall, 1984), 162.

21. Harry Eckstein, "On the Etiology of Internal Wars," in *History and Theory* IV, 133-163.

22. *Latinos and the Los Angeles Uprising: The Economic Context,* 6.

23. *Daily Bulletin,* February 11, 1993.

24. *Latinos and the Los Angeles Uprising: The Economic Context,* 9.

25. *Los Angeles Times*, May 13, 1993.

26. *Ibid.*

27. *Los Angeles Times*, May 8, 1992.

28. *Ibid.*

29. *Ibid.*

30. *Ibid.*

31. *Los Angeles Times*, July 24, 1992.

32. *Los Angeles Times*, December 13, 1992.

33. *Los Angeles Times*, July 10, 1992.

34. Danny Blackwell's article came out in the *Los Angeles Times* on July 8, 1992. Xavier Hermosillo's article followed on July 9, 1992. Numerous articles followed on the rift between the two leaders during the summer months of 1992.

35. *Los Angeles Times*, July 22, 1992.

36. *Los Angeles Times*, September 15, 1992.

37. *Ibid.*

38. *Los Angeles Times*, May 18, 1992.

39. *Ibid.*

40. *Riverside Enterprise Times,* July 16, 1993.

41. *Los Angeles Times,* August 24, 1992.

42. *Los Angeles Times,* July 13, 1993.

43. *Los Angeles Times*, October 27, 1992.
44. *Los Angeles Times*, June 16, 1992.
45. *Daily Bulletin*, July 12, 1993.

Race, Class, Conflict and Empowerment:
On Ice Cube's
"Black Korea"

JEFF CHANG

I. Locating the Spaces of Struggle

Amidst the tempest between Du Soon Ja's conviction and sentencing in late 1991, Los Angeles rap artist Ice Cube issued a brutally terse fictional judgment of his own on a song called "Black Korea." With an audio snippet from Spike Lee's *Do The Right Thing*, he placed himself as a customer in a Korean American-owned corner store trying to purchase a forty-ounce bottle of malt liquor. What should have been a simple transaction was about to become another aggravating experience.

As the music bursts forth, the scene is set for an ugly confrontation. Ice Cube confronts two prejudiced, "Oriental, one penny counting" proprietors. They follow him suspiciously as he walks through their store. Their close scrutiny infuriates the rapper, who turns and leers at the woman storekeeper, "Bitch, I got a job." At the song's bridge, the shop erupts into argument when his friends raise their voices in his support.

By now the original Spike Lee scene has been transformed, fully stripped of all its irony and humor, left with only the raw racial conflict. Then the heavy bass surges back and the song rushes along to its pitched conclusion. First Ice Cube issues an economic threat, "Don't follow me up and down your crazy little market, or your little chop suey ass will be the target of a nationwide boycott." In a final defiant

---

JEFF CHANG is a graduate student in UCLA's Asian American Studies M.A. program.

gesture, he raises the prospect of a racially vengeful conflagration. "Pay respect to the black fist," he yells, "or we'll burn your store right down to a crisp, and then we'll see ya because you can't turn the ghetto into Black Korea." The Korean store-owner has the last word: "Mother fuck *you*!"

Tension between African Americans and Asian Americans is a subtext running throughout the album, entitled *Death Certificate*, which finds Ice Cube partially repudiating his previous street gangster pose and replacing it with an emerging nationalist perspective. But his new embrace of blackness comes with an antipathy for Asians. On "Horny Lil' Devil," a track about black male emasculation, he gets so energized from wiping out the "devils" (variously seen as white sexual harassers of black women, racists, and "fags") that he runs around to the corner store to beat up the "Jap" owner. On "Us," he fumes at "sellouts" and calls for black racial solidarity when he sees "Japs grabbing every vacant lot in my 'hood to build a store and sell they goods."

Ice Cube's comments on Asians were not a new development in hip hop music. Dating to the 1990 Red Apple Grocery boycott in the Flatbush section of Brooklyn, rap sometimes served as a forum for young urban blacks to express their feelings on tensions related to Asian Americans. Queen Mother Rage, a rapper affiliated with Sonny Carson's Blackwatch Movement, denounced "the Orientals hungry for each piece of our prize." On a single called "To Be Real," she cautioned, "Check the incidents and the innocence. Ignorance is no defense." Special Ed's teen rewrite of a James Bond fantasy, "The Mission," found the young rapper traveling to Japan to confront a Chinese nemesis. When he discovers that his enemy not only possesses amazing "black belt karate" skills but also catches bullets in his teeth, Ed gets down and defeats his opponent "Flatbush style." (Conflation of very different Asian American cultural identities into a new myth of a threatening, as opposed to a model, minority was a recurrent theme.) And during the hot, tense summer months, Chubb Rock led a New York concert crowd in chants of "Fuck you, eggroll."

These created musical spaces of struggle arose from real urban spaces of increasing racial strife. In South Central Los Angeles, for example, a number of large plant closings contributed to a black male jobless rate of about fifty percent in some areas.[1] The poverty rate of Asians in Los Angeles County grew to twice that of whites, while the poverty rates for Blacks and Latinos each swelled past three times that of whites.[2] At the same time, the succession of Korean immigrants into small businesses in the South Central Los Angeles area created a new ethnic petit bourgeoisie or a "middleman minority."[3] The convergence of these factors set the context for new conflict and tensions between Korean and African Americans that were only beginning to peak at the start of the nineties. In 1991, three firebombings of Korean American stores took place during the month of August alone. By 1992, a survey of racial attitudes in Los Angeles conducted before and just after the April uprising showed that more than 41 percent of Blacks and 48 percent of Asians felt that it was difficult to get along with the other group. Blacks felt *worse* about Asians after the riots. Asians, too, saw Blacks more negatively.[4]

Ice Cube's one-minute long rap was a highly concentrated summation and evocation of interracial conflict in a environment of deteriorating opportunities. But it was also an artifact of popular culture. The *Death Certificate* album went to number two on the *Billboard* charts a week after it was released and went on to sell over one and a half million copies. The album's explosive content ignited a searing debate in the mass media. Feeling substantially and materially targeted, Korean American community leaders and grocers initiated economic boycotts against Ice Cube's album and the St. Ides malt liquor that he endorsed. Thus a musical work was transformed into a political cause.

The impact of "Black Korea," in particular, represents a moment where issues of interracial conflict and political empowerment crystallized in a clash of what Edward Chang calls "strategies of survival" for Asian Americans and African Americans.[5] The struggle for group power, the power to shape and influence given situations to maximal outcomes, was waged on two fronts: on the media front for social-political power and the market front for economic-political power. African and Asian Americans employed tactics and strategies consistent with their resources, and consonant to their objectives. This article looks at how the hierarchy of racial power in the media and in the marketplace shaped the dynamics of the conflicts.

For African and Asian Americans, power shifted slightly in different contexts. The media debate reveals how "Black Korea" was received by various audiences. Interpretations of the song varied widely because of the positions of its different audiences by class, generation, and social power. Yet not all interpretations were equally covered. While whites and blacks held a one-sided debate over the merits of Ice Cube's work, the marginality of Korean American opinion reflected Asian American social-political disempowerment. Racial groups also acted and reacted upon material readings of the song. Korean Americans saw the boycotts as strategies for political empowerment. At the same time, the success of the grocers' boycott success was not received well by some members of the African American community. They saw such success as proof of African

Americans' economic-political disempowerment. But neither African nor Asian American tactics and strategies yielded substantial gains to their respective groups.

On spaces of struggle such as South Central Los Angeles, political organizing to expand minority access and power has become increasingly complex and movements seem increasingly and inevitably to be drawn into collision courses with each other. Community organizations attempting to empower communities of color have drawn on two coexisting and sometimes compatible, but basically divergent approaches to organizing. Both an anti-colonial approach, which seeks a unity of racially colonized peoples against a white ruling class, and a nationalist approach, which seeks racial solidarity for collective group advancement, appear as problematic here. I suggest utilizing a recognition of "differential disempowerment" as a way of reducing opposition between disempowered racial groups and creating new space for those groups to move towards full access and participation.

II. But You Don't Hear Me Though:
RACIAL POWER IN CRITICAL INTERPRETATION

Mass culture theorists have criticized audiences for popular culture as an ignorant horde brought together by their low tolerance for style, subtlety and significance, their need for instant gratification, their blind submission to commodification and their passive acceptance of demagoguery masquerading as culture. Theodor Adorno called popular music "a social cement" which strips listeners of their individuality and binds them by their psychological needs. Youth are seen as particularly prone to becoming literal "slaves to the rhythm."[6]

Yet this analysis is inadequate to understanding the impact "Black Korea" had on its well over one-and-a-half-million listeners. Many scholars see audiences not as passive subjects but as creators of their own political meanings.[7] Dick Hebdige, for example, explains punk music and style as a calculated subcultural act of "noise," which he defines as "interference in the orderly sequence which leads from real events and phenomena to their representation in the media."[8] Rather than support authoritarian power, he concludes, punks use their subculture to actively resist it. By exploring punk music from its audience's perspective, Hebdige is able to dissect power and ideology. Such an approach highlights who shapes discourse about popular culture, how that discourse is shaped and what that discourse says.

Rap music's appeal has grown to include white suburban, Latina/o, and female audiences. The focus here is confined to three distinct (if not completely homogenous) audiences: the black rap music audience, the mainstream white media, and the Asian American audience. I look at how these audiences reacted critically to "Black Korea" and also to other audiences' reactions. I also examine where these audiences voiced their opinions. By looking at ideology and representation, it is possible to arrive at a hierarchy of social-political power.

Hip hop is an American subculture developed by marginalized African American and Puerto Rican youth in New York ghettoes during the seventies. The subculture encompasses spray can art and street dancing, and rapping is part of its musical branch. As David Toop has shown, rapping fits into a cultural line that can be traced back through the African American historical experience to the pre-slavery West African oral tradition.[9] Thus one of rap music's many functions is to continue the long rich line of African American social protest and commentary. The modern popularization and commodification of African American music has transformed but not significantly altered this basic cultural function.

African American audiences for rap music, overwhelmingly young audiences, played the central role in the legitimization of Ice Cube from his early days as a "gangsta" hero to his rise to a kind of modern-day *griot* status. They formed his core audience when he was rhyming, "To a kid looking up to me, life ain't nothing but bitches and money."[10] Later in his career, after two platinum albums and success among white "crossover" audiences, they stood by him strongly during the controversy over "Death Certificate." Many fended off criticism of his work by claiming his work as representative of their own experiences and by suggesting his detractors were motivated by racism.

Angela Griffin wrote in the *Los Angeles Sentinel*, "Since Cube is trying to kick it on the positive side, trying to wake us up to the conspiracy against Blacks, and how the White man is both brainwashing and using us so we can ruin each other, someone wants to cause an uproar. Why? Because they're getting scared. They don't want us to realize what they're trying to do—capture us in a mental slavery."[11]

James Bernard, senior editor of hip hop magazine *The Source*, defended Ice Cube against calls for boycotts, "Yes, Ice Cube is very angry, and he expresses that anger in harsh, blunt, and unmistakable terms. But the source of his rage is very real. Many in the black community, particularly Los Angeles, Cube's home, feel as if it's open season on blacks with the Rodney King assault and the recent murder of a young black girl by a Korean merchant."[12]

For many disenfranchised youth of all colors, but primarily African Americans, hip hop subculture is a stylistic revolt against limited economic opportunities and racial prejudice. At the same time, it sometimes converts peer group competition into violent metaphor. Real or invented enemies are routinely and mercilessly slaughtered in the record grooves. "Gangsta" rap can be compared to the highly popular film genre of action-adventure movies. As Gina Marchetti writes,

> Particular genres tend to be popular at certain points in time because they somehow embody and work through those social contradictions the culture needs to come to grips with and may not be able to deal with except in the realm of fantasy. As such, popular genres often function the way myth functions-to work through social contradictions in the form of a narrative so that very real problems can be transposed to the realm of fantasy and apparently solved there.[13]

In a context of limited social opportunity for African American youth, the popularity of "gangsta" rap and the iconization of "hardcore" gangsta rappers makes sense, even if one thinks muscial "gangsta"-ism is not sensible. "Gangsta" rappers argue that their poetry mirrors their reality. But these raps function as more than mirrors, they are also self-myth-making.

In "Black Korea," Ice Cube's attempts to move from 'hood hero to "race man" by taking the "us" versus "them" dialectic into the realm of interracial relations. He has stated that the song "holds the tone of the neighborhood and the feelings of the people."[14] He has also remarked:

> . . .it's inspired by everyday life in the black community with the Koreans. Blacks don't like them and it's vice versa. The Koreans have a lot of businesses in the black community. The (Harlins) shooting is just proof of the problem, just another example of their disrespect for black people. You go in their stores and they think you're going to steal something. They follow you around the store like you're a criminal. They say, "Buy something or get out." If it hasn't happened to you, you can't know how bad it feels for somebody to make you feel like a criminal when you're in their store and you haven't done anything.[15]

The fiery conclusion of "Black Korea" is understood by many of Cube's African American fans in the 'hood for its mythical, metaphorical resolution of the very real social problems of economic disenfranchisement, Korean American prejudice, and interracial conflict. Although rappers often claim their rhymes are a form of poetic journalism, this is beside the point. The music's liberation comes in its transposing of the real-life problems into terms that can be controlled.

When the debate over the merits of Ice Cube's record erupted, African American music critics quickly rose to his defense in black newspapers across the country, as well as in the large urban network of hip hop magazines. African American audiences also represented themselves in response to mainstream editorials. Chuck D of the rap group Public Enemy and Bernard were given prominent space in *Billboard Magazine* to challenge the apparent anti-black media bias.[16] Hip hop music itself, a space where culture and subculture converge and assert, functions as representation, as what Hebdige calls "noise."[17] Ice Cube devoted the lead cut of his next album *The Predator* to answering *Billboard's* charges.[18] Yet whites still ultimately shaped the parameters within which African Americans could respond. As Coco Fusco cautioned, one could not "confuse the appearance of access created by the commodification of ethnicity...with the decentralization of wealth and democratization of political power that have yet to take place in this country."[19]

On the other hand, Asian American listeners were left largely muted in the debate. They found their voices largely limited to the ethnic press, especially the *Korea Times* of Los Angeles, *Asian Week* and the alternative music press. Korean Americans were not quoted in any kind of mainstream news coverage until after the grocers' boycott concluded. Young Koreans, in particular, expressed strong but conflicting and contradictory emotions. Michael Park, an Asian American rapper and a community activist in Seattle, was a good example. He had been a victim, along with his brother and two black friends, in a celebrated incident of police brutality at the campus of the University of Washington.[20] A devotee of Ice Cube's earlier records, he nonetheless reacted strongly to "Black Korea."

"Not only is Cube offensive to Koreans and Korean Americans," Park wrote in the *Korea Times* of Los Angeles, "he has attacked Asian people as a whole."[21] He went on to ask the Korean community to use the incident to reflect on its own prejudices towards African Americans and expressed support for the boycotts. High school student Henry Yun argued that "Black Korea" was "a death threat to all Korean American merchants in this country," but also reported that most of his friends felt Ice Cube should not be banned.[22] In an attempt to "move away from the issue of censorship and the stereotyping of rap as violent and move toward addressing the core problem," Dong Suh, the son of a grocer, contributed a deeply emotional and articulate analysis of the tensions between Korean and African Americans.[23] Suh stated at the beginning of his piece,

> Several years ago, a prominent radio personality in Philadelphia, where my family operates a small corner store in a predominantly African American neighborhod, expressed a similar sentiment. I clearly remember his warning that if Koreans did not respect Blacks, firebombings were likely. Although it's hard not to react personally

to such statements, the problem lies neither with that radio personality nor with Ice Cube. His statement is merely a symptom of a more systematic problem that goes beyond the tension between African and Korean Americans. [24]

Suh also discussed the realities of social-political power in the 'hood, "When compared to Korean Americans, African Americans are a numerical and political majority. (Ice Cube) does not realize that as a member of the majority, he wields real power against Koreans."[25] He cut to the central issue for Asian American audiences when he tried to square "Black Korea"'s implied threat to material reality with the real issue of interracial conflict.

Korean American community leaders struggled with this quandary as well. Jerry Yu, executive director of the Korean American Coalition (KAC), stated, "Ice Cube kept saying that this is social commentary. And I think it's true, he's expressing a certain sentiment that's out there. But. . .not everybody might understand; some people might take it that he's encouraging or advocating violence against Korean store-owners."[26]

They also recognized that tensions were increasing in October and November of 1991, as they waited for the Du sentencing and tried to complete negotiations with African American activists who were boycotting another liquor store where an African American had been shot by a store owner. Eventually they were moved to action by what they perceived to be the political and material issues at stake. Yu felt it was irrelevant to discuss Ice Cube's free speech rights. Rather he stated, "We're talking about a moral obligation. When there's people in a position to affect a nationwide audience, they have a higher standard of responsibility to be fair, not to be discriminatory, or racist, or inflammatory, or to incite riots."[27] Yumi Jhang-Park, then the executive director of the Korean American Grocers' Association (KAGRO), publicly stated, "This is a life-and-death situation. What if someone listened to the song and set fire to a store?"[28]

But Korean American activists were unable to reach the mainstream press with their message. When *Entertainment Tonight* interviewed Yu regarding the boycott, they videotaped him for over thirty minutes. But the subsequent airing only featured him briefly, reading lyric excerpts from "Black Korea." On the other hand, Rabbi Abraham Cooper of the Los Angeles-based Jewish human-rights group, the Simon Wiesenthal Center, was shown explaining the boycott for most of the segment.[29] Again, the white mainstream media shaped the debate over "Black Korea."

Most mainstream media coverage took place on the music pages, but two political magazines also commented on rap on their news pages. White males created a defining perspective: they examined "Black Korea" in terms of whether its content required censorship.[30] *Los Angeles Times* rock critic Robert Hilburn set the stage in *Death Certificate*'s first review, stating, "Ice Cube. . .continues to make albums that spark debates over just how far pop music should go in chronicling frustration and rage."[31] The debate became greatly sharpened three weeks later in a controversial *Billboard Magazine* editorial. In calling for record store chains to consider boycotting the record, editor Timothy White wrote, "His unabashed espousal of violence against Koreans, Jews, and other whites crosses the line that divides art from the advocacy of crime."[32] In an industry magazine which usually ignored issues of artistic merit or lyrical content in its editorials, the editorial was extraordinary. *Death Certificate* remains the only album ever singled out for condemnation in *Billboard* history.

"Black Korea" even inspired political magazines not usually known for comment on "low" popular culture to comment on the apparent threat of rap music to society. An article in *The Economist* recalled Adorno's criticism of popular music, evoking "rhythmically obedient" but uncritical fans. "In rap as in rock, rebellion sells," the editorial read. "Sadly, too few fans distinguish between the rebellious and the reactionary."[33]

David Samuels, writing in *The New Republic*, also depicted rap fans as passive, mindless consumers, "This kind of consumption—of racist stereotypes, of brutality toward women, or even of uplifting tributes to Dr. Martin Luther King—is of a particularly corrupting kind. The values it instills find their ultimate expression in the ease in which we watch young black men killing each other: in movies, on records, and on streets of cities and towns across the country."[34] Thus, the other defining perspective in the "Black Korea" debate was whether or not being a rap fan constituted socially acceptable behavior.

Ideology and representation in the media reflected the hierarchy of social-political power, placing whites on top, African Americans far below, and Asian Americans still below them. Mainstream media focused coverage and commentary on "Black Korea" around themes of censorship and rebellion. Yet these themes were phrased in terms of a white-black racial axis; Koreans were useful to the discussion only insofar as they represented non-black targets of black rage. No one bothered to ask how Korean Americans might feel about the record. While Jewish boycott leaders were widely quoted, only two journalists felt obliged to quote a Korean American and they did so only after the grocers' boycott had ended.[35] At the same time, many liberal music critics felt they had to qualify their criticism of the record to African Americans by addressing their status position as white males.[36] White males shaped the ideological parameters for discussion. From there, they marginalized African American views by allowing response rather than representation and they marginalized Asian American views by largely denying representation.

III. Paying Respect to the Black Fist?:

The "Black Korea" Boycotts As A Strategy for Empowerment

Upon its release on October 31, 1991, *Death Certificate* had advance orders of over a million copies, making it an instant national hit. Yet the controversy around the album's content transformed the musical piece into a political issue. The rap which had threatened, "Don't follow me up and down your crazy little market or your lil' chop suey ass will be a target," became the central reason to target the rapper.

On November 1, the associate dean of the Simon Wiesenthal Center called upon four major retail record chains to boycott the album, calling it a "a cultural Molotov cocktail" and "a real threat."[37] Guardian Angels began pickets in New York and Los Angeles at record stores carrying the album. Two days later, the Korean American Coalition (KAC) held its own press conference, issuing a joint statement signed by the Japanese American Citizens League, the Los Angeles Urban League, the NAACP, the Mexican American Legal Defense and Educational Fund, and the Southern Christian Leadership Conference. Some Korean swap meet vendors and the Camelot Music chain also honored the boycott.[38]

The core of the KAC boycott was to challenge the representational problems. Yu said, "In the minds of Korean Americans, this is all part of the oppression or unfairness we face. We're constantly trampled on, nobody listens to us, we're constantly seen through distorted images in the media. . .We're not really battling against Ice Cube, all we're trying to do is get him to understand our concerns, get him to respond to our issues."[39] The boycott was in line with KAC's ongoing campaign against media stereotyping, which had included a boycott of the motion picture, *The Year of the Dragon*, and protests over racist coverage in *Time*, the *Los Angeles Times*, and *Rolling Stone*. But while the KAC boycott unleashed a flood of mail on the Priority Records offices, the record still went on to sell well over a million and a half records.

However, actions were also moving on a very different front. On November 7, the Korean American Grocers' Association (KAGRO) reached an impasse in negotiations with McKenzie River Corporation of San Francisco, the maker of the St. Ides Premium Malt Liquor for which Ice Cube was a prominent endorser. KAGRO had asked McKenzie River to withdraw all promotional materials and commercials featuring Ice·Cube and to sever its relationship with him. McKenzie River responded that meeting these demands would financially damage their small company and declined. KAGRO then initiated a campaign among its stores to return deliveries and cease orders for the malt liquor. Yang Il Kim, the national president of KAGRO, told the *Korea Times* that he had sympathy for McKenzie River's business worries, but he remained resolute on the boycott, noting that they picked the wrong rapper to endorse their beer.[40]

At its peak, between five and six thousand stores in Los Angeles, San Francisco, Oakland, San Jose, Seattle, Tacoma, Portland, Philadelphia, Baltimore, Richmond and Washington D.C. joined the campaign.[41] On November 16, McKenzie River broke down and conceded to KAGRO's demands, ending the use of all ads which featured Ice Cube and claiming it would not use him for new promotions. They also agreed to create a scholarship fund for black youths and a jobs program for black youth and adults from sales of St. Ides. KAGRO officially ended its boycott on November 20, only three weeks after the release of *Death Certificate*.[42]

Conciliation took place three months later. In early February, McKenzie River held a joint meeting between Ice Cube and the KAGRO leadership. Ice Cube apologized to the merchants and pledged to discourage violence against store owners and to continue "working to bring our communities closer together." In his letter to Kim, he wrote of the meeting:

> I explained some of the feelings and attitudes of black people today, and the problems and frustrations that we confront. And I clarified the intent of my album *Death Certificate*. It was not intended to offend anyone or to incite violence of any kind. It was not directed at all Korean Americans or at all Korean American store owners. I respect Korean Americans. It was directed at a few stores where my friends and I have had actual problems. Working together we can help solve these problems and build a bridge between our communities.[43]

KAGRO leaders expressed their pleasure with the meeting, conceding that Ice Cube had made some legitimate complaints and expressing hope that Blacks and Koreans would "help each other and learn to understand each other's cultures."[44]

Why was one economic boycott a failure and the other so successful? In the KAC boycott, Korean Americans lacked the social-political power to sustain a lasting impact. When asked about whether it might have been possible to mount the kind of protest that the police associations had against rapper Ice-T's song "Cop Killer," Yu argued, "There was no way we could organize that kind of impact."[45] He pointed out that the community's small size, the large number of recent immigrants, lack of voting strength, and economic self-interest prevented them from wielding a strong united front on this issue. KAC sought to gain legitimacy by working in concert with other civil rights organizations, incorporating the NAACP, the Mexican American Legal Defense and Education Fund, and the Simon Wiesenthal Center into the boycott. Yet as Lillian Matulic, Ice Cube's publicist, noted, "We received a lot of form letters. But in my opinion, the boycott would only affect the people who wouldn't listen to Ice Cube anyway."[46] The *Entertainment Tonight* fiasco was symbolic. KAC's boycott against media stereotypes failed partially because of a lack of media coverage. Asian American social-political power could not leverage the market.

However, KAGRO's use of market clout in its boycott of St. Ides was stunningly successful. Here the hierarchy of power changed, reversing the positions of African Americans and Asian Americans. If Korean Americans had been relatively disempowered in a social-political sense, they were, at least in this case, empowered in an economic-political sense. According to Executive Director Ryan Song, KAGRO represented over 3500 stores in Southern California alone, had over 20,000 members who generated $2 billion in annual sales, and controlled roughly 7% of the national market.[47] African American activists noted that McKenzie River Corporation was targeting a young, urban African American male audience by using rappers such as Ice Cube to sell their malt liquor.[48] The prospect of thousands of Korean grocers in their target areas returning their orders was clearly too much for the small company to bear. Yu argues that this shows race had little to do with the boycott, "It's not that the Korean American merchants are so much more powerful. St. Ides did not respond because they were Korean Americans, but because of the economic threat."[49] However, through the KAGRO boycott, Korean Americans were able to translate their status as small store-owners into ethnic economic-political empowerment.

Although the controversy over the song had ended, what Dong Suh called the core issues that created it had not gone away. Looking back a year later, Ice Cube told an interviewer:

> I live in the black community so I wanted to let the Korean community know the tension that we feel. You're in our neighborhoods, which is perfectly fine with me. I have no problem with that. But when we come into your store, you have to treat us with respect because we are putting your kids through college, we are putting food on your table and we deserve the same kind of respect of anybody that's going to the store. A lot of black people didn't feel that respect had been given or when the riots jumped off, Korean shops wouldn't have been a target.[50]

Many African Americans were outraged at the 1991 resolution of KAGRO's St. Ides boycott, tying it to the light sentencing of Soon Ja Du in the murder of Latasha Harlins, which had taken place only five days before. Sonny Carson, the leader of New York-based Blackwatch Movement and an organizer of previous boycotts against Korean stores, called for a one-day moratorium on the purchase of Korean-sold goods and services on Martin Luther King, Jr. Day, telling the *New York Amsterdam News*,

> We buy fruits, leather, jewelry, they sell us vegetables, repair our shoes, dry clean our clothes but they have no respect for us. We should spend money with people who respect us, not those who shoot us down. . .we will not tolerate their endorsement of murder in L.A. or anyplace else because that is what their boycott infers.[51]

If this seemed to be an extreme position from an activist thought by many to be opportunistic in engaging confrontation with Asian Americans, it was nonetheless an opinion shared by many other progressive African Americans. Sheena Lester of the *Los Angeles Sentinel* wrote an editorial angrily excoriating McKenzie River Corporation and KAGRO:

> Mind you, this is the same beer company. . .who shrugged off Black folks' complaints about those offensive St. Ides radio ads. . .These are the same weasels who now are bowing to the demands of insensitive, poison-pushing merchants, who are apparently more outraged about being called names than they are about a dead Black child. . .As for KAGRO, I s'pose it's business as usual for them, too—back to following us 'county recips'[52] around their respective stores, awaiting the opportunity to catch us being the untamed, non-civilized mongrels we are, right?[53]

Lester brought together the Du sentencing, the issue of alcoholism in the African American community, and the lack of black-owned stores in a diatribe against Korean American prejudice and their relative economic empowerment. For her, the resolution of the boycott was yet another example of African Americans being stepped upon by everyone.[54]

Even noted Berkeley professor and columnist Julianne Malveaux told a conference of black scholars in December of 1991,

> (Ice Cube) is saying what we all feel. Where is there space for us in this economy? Where is there space for us in this society? Can you value my life? A Korean woman—and this is not race-bashing—got off with five-hundred hours of community service for killing a fifteen-year-old black girl. Community service! Give me a break. And Los Angeles is about to pop right now.[55]

Whether or not Malveux was indeed race-baiting, Los Angeles finally "popped" on April 29, 1992, leaving the charred shells of Korean liquor stores as proof of the currency of her sentiments for certain South Central residents.

The boycotts were seen by its leaders as a method of empowering the Korean American community. Yu stated, "By expressing how we feel, we are making constant progress towards being equals in this society."[56] However, these goals were complicated by the role that class played in Korean American ethnic interests. KAGRO national president Kim recognized such problems when he told the *Korea Times* during the boycott, "We're trying to negotiate not to expand tensions."[57] Even after the boycott was over, the *Washington Post* portrayed Kim as sincerely trying to avoid further conflict. He was quoted as conceding that the rapper was not condemning the entire Korean American community, but only a few merchants, and was shown pleading with the writer , "I personally ask you to make a good article, a good comment between the communities."[58]

The question of where to place inner-city Korean American grocers in a class framework is difficult to adequately answer. The prevalent view is that Korean American grocers represent a "middleman minority," a small, distinct cultural group located between the wealthy elites and the subordinate majority. As the providers of goods and services, Korean Americans constitute a petit bourgeoisie. As recent immigrants, they inevitably come to feel their marginal social status when the poor majority comes to target them for social and economic complaints in political discourse and individual acts of hostility.[59] Edna Bonacich argues that immigrant and ethnic entrepreneurs are actually "cheap labor," exploited by capitalists just as workers are.[60] Most Korean small business owners do not make large profits and face a grueling host of difficulties, not the least of which is the constant threat of violent crime. Yet Bonacich and Light find that, as a "petit bourgeoisie," Korean Americans are likely to act like "quintessential capitalists with respect to their clients" who will "provide whatever service or commodity will sell" and who would take little interest in the "impact of their businesses on that community."[61] They find that the nature of their exploitation is much different from the exploitation of "local workers and the "local poor."[62]

As many have noted, Asian Americans in this position maintain ethnic and class solidarities that are difficult to separate.[63] While organizing around representational issues, organizers may not have taken into account the important class issues. KAC saw "Black Korea" as part of a line of racist, stereotypical portrayals of Korean Americans. Yu stated,

> What I'm trying to say is that what's right is right and what's wrong is wrong. So if someone is spouting hate and violence or something, and I'm not saying that Ice Cube necessarily did that, but if someone is calling for violence against a certain group, then it's wrong. No matter

who that person is, whether that person is black, white, Asian, Korean, whoever, it's wrong.[64]

Korean American attorney T.S. Chung was quoted in the *Korea Times* as saying that *Death Certificate* "reflects an attitude urging blacks to take the law into their own hands by burning down stores if they don't like the store owners. I don't think that is the kind of society we want to have."[65] Unfortunately, these statements could be read as suggesting that "Black Korea" represented the threat of racial conflict and not of class conflict, a "spin" on Black-Korean tensions used often by the white mainstream media. This cultural cul-de-sac of an argument appears only to open into a downward spiral into violence, flattening the complexities of the situation by painting African Americans the racial aggressor and Korean Americans the racial victim, covering over real economic issues with inflammatory racial overtones.

In the same press conference, Chung went on to say that although there was "some justifiable anger. . .Koreans didn't have anything to do with the creation of that situation."[66] Undeniably, in the zero-sum game of racial struggle in the ghetto, neither Korean Americans nor African Americans were successful in empowering themselves. They found themselves on an isolated space, thrown into battle, fighting for no real prize. Yu characterized the boycotts' end in this manner, "No way do I see it as a victory. If there was a victory, it would have been that he wouldn't have released the album in the first place."[67]

IV. Finding and Defining Common Ground

Professor Manning Marable, writing for the *Korea Times of New York,* called for African American self-criticism in regards to Ice Cube and boycotts of Korean stores. In doing so, he also eloquently summed up the difficulty of finding a common ground amidst shrinking resources. He stated:

> Certainly, Ice Cube reflects much of the righteous anger and hostility of our people. . .But to target our anger against Asian Americans does not, in the long run, resolve the crisis of poverty, economic oppression and a lack of Black ownership, which is the consequence of a racist, corporate system. Attacking petty entrepreneurs who are also people of color only permits those who directly benefit from the oppression of both groups to get away unscathed. The second problem presented by Ice Cube's lyrics involves the promise of a truly progressive Rainbow Coalition. People of color must transcend the terrible tendency to blame each other, to emphasize their differences, to trash one another.[68]

How are we to transcend? We may need first to revisit our primary assumptions on political organizing.

An anti-colonial approach has guided progressive people of color for three decades. This approach is rooted in the idea that racial minorities in America are, and have historically been, colonized peoples who share a similar situation of oppression and because of which have a common natural unity against the white colonizers.[69] Yet this approach has been made problematic by immigration policy and demographic shifts. Within Asian American communities, class stratification and ethnic difference appear to have increased since the 1965 Immigration Act. In inner-city spaces like South Central Los Angeles, race and class work together in creating a situation of tension and unrest between Asian Americans and African Americans.[70]

Korean and other Asian Americans may form a petit bourgeoisie able to exploit an African American and Latino poor. In Donald Noel's conception, this situation meets two of the three criteria to establish ethnic stratification: ethnocentrism and competition over scarce resources. The third criteria is the establishment of power by one group over another. Until this occurs, Noel argues there will be a destabilizing conflict.[71] Edward Chang argues similarly, "In the Korean-black relationship, the dominant-subordinate position has not been established between the two groups. When the perceived or real power of two groups is equal, or if each group believes that it is superior over the other group, there is a high probability for violent and direct confrontation."[72]

Political empowerment must therefore be examined closely. If Asian Americans extend their economic power to include social-political power over African Americans, the situation in South Central Los Angeles may stabilize at the cost of ethnic stratification. At the same time, Asian American marginality in the "rebuild Los Angeles" process demonstrate that the costs of disempowerment are far too serious.[73] But if a simple white-nonwhite axis of the anticolonial approach is increasingly difficult to apply in a multiracial environment, a purely nationalist approach is also problematic. This approach depends upon an ethnic-nonethnic axis, calling for empowerment through organizing for a limited ethnic solidarity.

The Blackwatch Movement's one-day moratorium on Korean goods hoped to symbolically demonstrate to African Americans that their interests can only be served by their own. But such tactics beg the question of whether resources might be better spent in starting up black-owned businesses and from where the capital to start up such businesses would come. On the other hand, KAGRO's nationalism provided a different set of problems. Yang Il Kim's dilemma was how to prevent a possible backlash from African Americans. By downplaying the resolution of the boycott (the meeting with Ice Cube was not reported for three months and then only as a balance to the traumatic riot headline "Cry Koreatown"), he was forced to snatch defeat from the jaws of a pyrrhic victory.

Especially on spaces abandoned and left to communities of color, it is not realistic to hope to promote the interests of one group without the other. Binary oppositions of white and nonwhite or ethnic and nonethnic must be recast in more complex approaches to understanding power. Michael Omi argues for an understanding of "differential racialization" to help explain how class affects a diverse Asian American experience.[74] Similarly, a notion of "differential forms of disempowerment" amongst communities of color might help organizers and public policy analysts grapple with complex interracial conflicts. Growing multiplicities of race and culture, further complicated by class, argue for a focus on where and for whom power lies and where and for whom it does not. This analysis must also be situational; it would be an obvious mistake to assume the hierarchies found in South Central Los Angeles apply everywhere. History, space, and context shape power relations and the attempts to redistribute power.

For Asian Americans, it is no longer (if it ever was) enough to claim similarity and solidarity with African Americans, difference and divergence must be acknowledged. In discussing alternative jurisprudential methods, Mari Matsuda argues:

> Our various experiences are not co-extensive. I cannot pretend that I, as a Japanese American, truly know the pain of, say, my Native American sister. But I can pledge to educate myself so that I do not receive her pain in ignorance.[75]

Matsuda warns Asian Americans against allowing themselves to "be used" by whites against other groups of color.[76] Asian Americans must work with other communities to mitigate points of difference and minimize points of tension.

Calls for multiracial unity and cross-cultural understanding without an understanding of the specific ways in which relative power is manifested and used can become pointless exercises. Claims to empowerment can become tools to maintain historical forms of subordination. We cannot move forward until we are more aware in our movements of the different paths that have brought each of us to this common space. Only then can we take the steps we must take to shaping and sharing our spaces in common.

Notes

My deepest appreciation to Kyeyoung Park, Russell Leong, Edward Chang, Mary Kao, the UCLA Asian American Studies and Afro-American Studies Reading Rooms, Bill Adler, Marcy Morgan, Ben Kim, Michael Park, Adisa Banjoko, Sheena Lester, Jerry Yu, Lillian Matulic, Nate Santa Maria, Joseph Ahn and the URB massive.

1. James Johnson, Cloyzelle K. Jones, Walter Farrell, and Melvin Oliver, "The Los Angeles Rebellion, 1992: A Preliminary Assessment From

Ground Zero," UCLA *Center for the Study of Urban Poverty, Occasional Working Paper Series* 2:7 (Los Angeles: UCLA Center for the Study of Urban Poverty, May 1992), 6.

2. The Research Group on the Los Angeles Economy, *The Widening Divide: Income Inequality and Poverty in Los Angeles* (Summary of Findings). (Los Angeles: UCLA Graduate School of Architecture and Urban Planning), 8.

3. On Korean Americans, see: Ivan Light and Edna Bonacich, *Immigrant Entrepreneurs: Koreans In Los Angeles, 1965-1982*, (Berkeley: University of California Press, 1988); Kyeyoung Park, "Placing the Korean Petit Bourgeoisie in the Los Angeles Crisis: The Interpenetration of Race and Class," unpublished paper (1993.) For recent work on the "middleman minority" theory applicable to Asian Americans, see: Turner, Jonathan H. and Edna Bonacich, "Toward A Composite Theory of Middleman Minorities." *Ethnicity* 7(1980): 144-158; Bonacich, Edna and John Modell, *The Economic Basis of Ethnic Solidarity: Small Business in the Japanese American Community*, (Berkeley, California: University of California Press, 1980.)

4. Lawrence Bobo, James Johnson, Melvin Oliver, James Sidanius, and Camille Zubrinsky, "Public Opinion Before And After A Spring of Discontent," *UCLA Center for the Study of Urban Poverty, Occasional Working Paper Series* 3:1 (Los Angeles, California: UCLA Center for the Study of Urban Poverty, September 1992), tables C27 and C28.

5. Edward Tea Chang, "New Urban Crisis: Korean-Black Conflicts in Los Angeles." Ph.D. dissertation, Ethnic Studies, (Berkeley, California: University of California at Berkeley, 1990): 23.

6. Theodor Adorno, "On Popular Music" in *On Record: Rock, Pop and the Written Word*, edited by Simon Frith and Andrew Goodwin, (New York: Pantheon Books, 1990): 311-312. See also: Herbert Gans, "Popular Culture in America: Social Problem in a Mass Society or Social Asset in a Pluralist Society?" in *Social Problems: A Modern Approach*, edited by Howard S. Becker, (New York: John Wiley and Sons, 1966): 549-620.

7. Simon Frith, "Music For Pleasure," *Screen Education* 34 (Spring 1980): 53.

8. Dick Hebdige, *Subculture: The Meaning of Style*. (London and New York: Methuen, 1979): 90.

9. David Toop, *The Rap Attack 2: African Rap to Global Hip Hop*, (London and New York: Serpent's Tail, 1991): 19.

10. N.W.A., "Gangsta, Gangsta," on *Straight Outta Compton*, Ruthless Records Recording, 1988.

11. Angela Griffin, "The Iceman Cometh, And So Does The Controversy," *Los Angeles Sentinel*, December 5, 1991.

12. James Bernard in "'Death Certificate' Gives Birth To Debate," *Billboard*, December 7, 1991.

13. Gina Marchetti, "Action Adventure As Ideology," in *Cultural Politics In Contemporary America*, edited by Ian Angus and Sut Jhally, (New York and London: Routledge, 1989): 187.

14. Ice Cube interview tape, Priority Records, 1992.

15. Dennis Hunt, "Outrageous As He Wants To Be," *Los Angeles Times,* November 3, 1991.

16. *Billboard,* December 7, 1991.

17. Hebdige, 90.

18. The chorus of "The Predator" is a characteristically blunt, "Fuck Billboard and the editor. I am the Predator." Ice Cube, *The Predator,* Priority Records Recording, 1992.

19. Coco Fusco, "Pan-American Postnationalism," in *Black Popular Culture,* edited by Gina Dent (Seattle, Washington: Bay Press, 1992): 281.

20. Michael Park, "A Night of Terror," *Korea Times* (Los Angeles), April 24, 1991.

21. Michael Park, "Ice Cube stereotypes all Asians, not just Koreans," *Korea Times* (Los Angeles), January 20, 1992.

22. Henry Yun, "'Black Korea'" is a death threat," *Korea Times* (Los Angeles), November 11, 1991.

23. Dong Suh, "The Source of Korean and African American Tensions," *Asian Week,* February 21, 1992.

24. *Ibid.*

25. *Ibid.*

26. Author interview with Jerry Yu of Korean American Coalition, March 1993.

27. *Ibid.*

28. John Leland, "Cube on Thin Ice," *Newsweek* 118:69 (December 2, 1991): 69.

29. Yu to J. Chang.

30. See also: Robert Christgau, "Me And The Devil Blues," *Village Voice,* December 17, 1991; Dave Marsh, "Record Review of 'Death Certificate,'" *Playboy* 39:3 (March 1992); RJ Smith, "The Racist You Love To Hate," *Los Angeles Weekly* (November 15-21, 1992); Jon Pareles, "Tales From The Dark Side, Spun By A Reluctant Outlaw," *New York Times,* November 11, 1992; Jon Pareles, "Should Ice Cube's Voice Be Chilled?" *New York Times.,* December 8, 1991; Joe Queenan, "Hate on Ice: Taking the Rap on Racism," *Washington Post,* December 29, 1991.

31. Robert Hilburn, "A Crucial Message, A Crude Delivery From Ice Cube," *Los Angeles Times,* November 3, 1991.

32. "Editorial," *Billboard,* November 23, 1991.

33. "Cracked Ice," *The Economist* 321: 7735 (November 30, 1991).

34. David Samuels, "The Rap on Rap," *New Republic,* November 11, 1991, 29. Certainly Samuel's reference to Dr. King seems ironic. Yet it seems to me no irony was intended. His position contrasts with Coco Fusco's.

35. Lynne Duke, "Rapper's Number Chills Black-Korean Relations," *Washington Post,* December 1, 1991, and Leland, 69.

36. In particular, see Christgau's piece on Ice Cube cited above.

37. Chuck Philips, "Wiesenthal Center Denounces Ice Cube's Album," *Los Angeles Times*, November 2, 1991.

38. Sophia Kyung Kim, "Chilling Fields: Ice Cube rap," *Korea Times* (Los Angeles), November 11, 1991.

39. Yu to J. Chang.

40. Richard Reyes Fruto, "KAGRO puts freeze on Ice Cube," *Korea Times* (Los Angeles), November 18, 1991.

41. Duke, A9.

42. Richard Reyes Fruto, "St. Ide's cans Ice Cube," *Korea Times* (Los Angeles), November 25, 1991.

43. Quoted in Sophia Kyung Kim, "Ice Cube the peacemaker," *Korea Times* (Los Angeles), May 4, 1992.

44. *Ibid.*

45. Yu to J. Chang.

46. Author interview with Lillian Matulic, publicist for Priority Records, March 1993.

47. Speech given by Ryan Song at "Conference on New Directions for the Korean-American Community," University of Southern California, March 1993.

48. Carla Marinucci, "Malt liquor's rapper ads changing tone." *San Francisco Examiner*, December 15, 1991.

49. Yu to J. Chang.

50. Interview of Ice Cube by Ruben Martinez, *Life and Times* TV show, originally aired on KCET Los Angeles, January 20, 1993.

51. Vinette K. Pryce, "Carson and 'Blackwatch' to boycott Koreans on MLK Day," *New York Amsterdam News*, 82: 52 (December 28, 1991).

52. A reference to welfare recipients in Ice Cube's "Us" on "Death Certificate": "Too much backstabbing/While I look out the window and see all the Japs grabbin'/Every vacant lot in my 'hood/ Build a store and sell they goods/To the county recips/You know us poor niggas/Nappy hair and big lips/Four, five kids on ya crotch and you expect Uncle Sam to help us out?"

53. Sheena Lester, "Youth Ideas Section: From the Editor." *Los Angeles Sentinel*, December 12, 1991.

54. Author interview with Sheena Lester, former Youth Ideas editor of the *Los Angeles Sentinel*, February 1993.

55. Julianne Malveux, "Popular Culture and the Economics of Alienation" in *Black Popular Culture*, edited by Gina Dent (Seattle: Bay Press, 1992): 207.

56. Yu to Chang.

57. Fruto, (November 18, 1991).

58. Duke, A9.

59. See: Bonacich and Modell, Turner and Bonacich.

60. Edna Bonacich, "The Social Costs of Immigrant Entrepreneurship." *Amerasia Journal* 14:1 (1988): 120. See also: Pyong Gap Min, "The Social Costs of Immigrant Entrepreneurship: A Response to Edna Bonacich." *Amerasia Journal* 15:2 (1989): 187-194. Edna Bonacich, "The Role of the Petite Bourgeoisie within Capitalism: A Response to Pyong Gap Min." *Amerasia Journal* 15:2 (1989): 195-203.

61. Light and Bonacich, 433-4.

62. Light and Bonacich, 366-370.

63. See: K. Park, Bonacich and Modell, (1988).

64. Yu to Chang.

65. S. Kim, November 11, 1991.

66. *Ibid.*

67. Yu to Chang.

68. Manning Marable, "Black prof sees America belonging to people of color, criticizes Ice Cube." Republished in *Korea Times* (Los Angeles), February 18, 1992.

69. Robert Blauner, *Racial Oppresion In America* (New York: Harper and Row, 1972), 52. See also: Albert Memmi, *The Colonizer and The Colonized* (Boston: Beacon Press, 1965); Stokely Carmichael and Charles Hamilton, *Black Power: The Politics of Liberation in America* (New York: Vintage Books, 1967).

70. K. Park, 5-7.

71. Donald Noel, "A Theory of the Origins of Ethnic Stratification." *Social Problems* 16:2 (Fall 1968): 157-172.

72. E. Chang, 28.

73. A 1993 study by the Korean American Inter-Agency Council shows that only 28 percent of the stores that were burned down are being rebuilt, testament to the limited reach of Korean American economic-political power. Elaine Kim shows the depth of Asian American social-political disempowerment in her discussion of her experience with *Newsweek* magazine. See: Elaine H. Kim, "Home is Where the Han Is: A Korean American Perspective on the Los Angeles Upheavals," *Social Justice* 20:1 (Spring, Summer 1993): 1-21.

74. Michael Omi, "Out of the Melting Pot and Into The Fire: Race Relations Policy," in *The State of Asian Pacific America*, edited by J. D. Hokoyama and Don Nakanishi (Los Angeles, California: LEAP Asian Pacific American Pubic Policy Institute and UCLA Asian American Studies Center, 1993): 207.

75. Mari Matsuda, "When the First Quail Calls: Multiple Consciousness as Jurisprudential Method," *Women's Rights Law Reporter* 11:1 (Spring 1989): 10.

76. Mari Matsuda, "We Will Not Be Used," From a speech given April 1990 at Asian Law Caucus. Reprinted in *Asian American Pacific Islands Law Journal* 1:1 (February 1993): 79-84.

Which Side Are You On?

The Rebellion Causes Pride and Pain for One Observer

Who Is Half Asian, Half Black

Arvli Ward

UCLA's Asian and Pacific Islander Newsmagazine   Volume 16   Issue 5   April 1992

I keep thinking back to a moment that occurred sometime after midnight on the first night of burning and looting. I am standing against a low wall at the edge of a parking lot near Florence and Vermont, watching people stream in and out of a trashed-up supermarket when two men pass me.

"Black power," one of them says in an offhand way.

It strikes me as a remarkable utterance. I am speechless for a moment. "Black power," I finally sputter. In my memory I see the moment punctuated—as if it were a scene out of a movie—by an exploding transformer box that lights up the undersky with a brilliant blue flash before casting the entire area into total darkness.

It was Black Power, wasn't it? This feeling in the soot-filled air. Deep in the African ghetto of Los Angeles where some of the city's poorest live, people are moving casually against property, that concept around which lives are wrapped in this free market world, taking what they please. Authority, in the form of the police, won't show anytime soon; it's clear that some institutions don't apply tonight.

Someone sits a few feet away from me smoking a cigarette and begins to tell it to no one in particular: "Niggas breaking up the slave quarters. . .looting the goods. . . overseerer can't do a damn thing about it. . ." From the handful assembled there comes chorus of chuckles, a murmur of agreement.

I thought of the Last Poets and their refrain: "Black day is coming. . .Black day is here." I can't deny the exhilaration I felt at that moment. I know I was raised better, but it was a glorious moment. It looked as if the revolution had arrived.

But my mind keeps returning to another moment, this one occurring about twelve hours later. In that moment, I see two faces I recognize as Japanese, though everyone else takes them for Korean. They are the faces of a middle-aged couple in a yellow Cadillac with white interior decorated with crocheted doilies. They are traveling west—out of the ghetto where they may live, perhaps behind the old Crenshaw Square in a manicured duplex—slowing to turn southward on La Cienega, when a bare-chested Crip wearing dickies, work gloves, and a bandana tied around his face bandit-style, rushes the car and throws a bottle of beer through the driver's side window. The old man takes the exploding window and bottle in the side of the head and neck. He keeps driving, hands clenched at the top of the wheel. His mouth is agape. He spits shards of glass from his lips. His wife cries out, takes out her handkerchief and begins to reach up to dab his bloody face. Just then, our eyes seem to meet. Does she recognize me, I wonder, as I recognize her? Her face is so much like my mother's, I imagine, and in her eyes I sense a question. I flinch and look away.

A year later, my memories of the forty-eight hours I roamed the burning city are dominated by images of love and suffering like these. I have since quit trying to make sense of them, because I can't make the choices necessary. How do you balance Jubilation Day, as the Rasta on 54th called it, with all the Asian ass-kicking you see? Or as James Jenkins, my boyhood friend, used to ask me: "Is you a Jap, or is you a nigga?"

My father was born in rural Georgia to the fifteen-year-old daughter of a sharecropper. From the little he told me about his early years, I fashioned together a picture that remains as remote to me as literature. There was a farm, just a mean patch of land, an anchor into penury. A childhood without shoes. There was a town, Elberton, whose status as the granite capital of Georgia ensured magnificent monuments to the Confederacy. My father left the farm, moved on to the city, and lived by his wits like many black men in this society. Soon he joined the Marines and shipped out for the Korean War to kill Koreans and Chinese in the name of freedom. Eventually he was stationed in Japan at a base on the beautiful inland sea that faces China and there he met my mother, the displaced daughter of a Kobe shopkeeper. Their courtship was carried out at the Bar Happy, where jazz-loving Japanese women and black servicemen mingled. They married a year later and soon afterwards were disowned by their families. My father died before he could square things with his relatives who continued to believe that it was Georgia anti-miscegenation laws and not their bigotry that kept him away. My mother's rapprochment was finally complete nearly forty years later, although the elder brother who removed her from the *koseki*—the Japanese family registry that would establish the racial purity of your pedigree— was too senile before his death to notice that she had come back.

My father eventually moved us to Southern California, where I grew up in the racially jumbled milieu of a military town. We were the children of enlisted Marines, the Black, white, Latino, Native American and Samoan poor who came from ghettos, farms, and factory towns to make up the lower ranks. We were crowded into the "Posole," a Chicano barrio and the only neighborhood where nonwhites were free to buy. We were a motley assortment, many of us half something, born at stations in the Philippines, Korea, Guam, Japan and wherever else they sent Marines. We grew up gray girls, black cholos, pop-locking Asians, but Black was the dominant esthetic, absorbing youth of all groups, and I grew up thinking I was Black.

When the 29th of last April arrived, I was already wondering—something I thought I had quit doing long ago—what it meant to be African, what it meant to be Asian. It began when I found myself in an argument on a flight from Washington D.C. to Memphis. Although I was in the practice of denying it, I had been through this many times before. This time it was with a member of the Black Freedom Fighters Coalition, or so his jacket, which was covered in epigrams and names from black history, said.

A few minutes into our flight, he noticed that I was reading

Shelby Steele's *The Content of our Character*. Since he asked, I started to tell him what I thought I understood of the conservative Steele's ideas. I couldn't abide by them, I told him, but I must have sounded like an asshole anyway. "Why do you clutter up your mind with all that stuff?" he asked, his voice dripping with drama like a preacher's.

For the next couple of hours he loomed over me, his large body spilling into my seat, and preached. He asked me what right I had to say I was Black. Yeah, I had black skin, he agreed, but I didn't sound Black, and if he had to guess, my ideas weren't very Black. At a couple of spots in the conversation, he'd pause and ask me: "You Filipino right?" It was meant as an insult, a reminder that what I claimed to be was irrelevant.

"It is people like you that will sell us out when the revolution comes," he said. At one point he challenged me to tell him who the people inscribed on his jacket were: Nat Turner, Bob Marley, Paul Robeson et al. When I proved up to the simple quiz, he looked at his girl and said: "You see what they throw at you?" She smiled knowingly.

What he meant was that I was a "race spy," someone who knew about being Black, but wasn't Black. I was a danger, a potential sellout stuck on succeeding at the expense of real black folks. Would I join the FBI, he asked, if I wasn't already in it?

He had found the button. Could he have known that all my life, I struggled for black acceptance, many times at the expense of my Asian side? Moments like these, long repressed and smoothed over in the making of my personal myth, sprang up. I was kissing his ass—in the same way I had done in these situations since I learned long ago what being half-black and half-Japanese meant— begging him to deem me worthy of being called a brother.

"Every brother ain't a brother," he told me, invoking Chuck D.

After a while, it got nasty. White folks started looking.

We landed and I switched seats in Memphis for the rest of the flight back to California. When he found out that I was moving to another seat, he stood up and looked back at me with an expression of utter disappointment and disgust.

He was right, and it was useless to argue: He was blacker than me.

And he may have been right about even more. Maybe I was a race spy, and perhaps that's why I felt no real allegiance to Africa or Japan, especially on the 29th as I watched the events. All I could do was celebrate the love and feel the suffering.

ARVLI WARD is the ASUCLA news-magazine adviser.
"Which Side Are You On?" is a reprint from *Pacific Ties* 16:5 (April 1993), 41, UCLA's Asian and Pacific Islander student newspaper. The article was part of a special issue "Remembering the L. A. Uprising One Year Later."

seoul
to
soul

Pictured above

(starting at upper right, clockwise):

Wanda Coleman, Lynn Manning,

Chungmi Kim, and Ko Won.

Digital Portraits by John Snyder.

Photographs in this section by Eugene Ahn.

GRAPHICS EDITOR: Mary Kao

Korean & African American Writers:
"Seoul To Soul"

MARI SUNAIDA

Introduction

Twelve years ago my brother returned from Seoul with his Korean fiancé, but the simple human pleasure of bringing home his future bride to meet his family was to be denied him as it had been denied my father and mother thirty years earlier. One would think that being first generation Asian women living in America would be common enough ground for my Japanese mother and my future sister-in-law to forge a bond. But the two women were wary of each other. Japan, after all, had occupied Korea. My brother had crossed the line—socially, historically, and politically. Never mind the fact that he was very much in love and that his Korean girlfriend was devoted to him. She sat at his feet and insisted on washing the dishes by herself which drove me and my sister who saw ourselves as liberated women crazy. Never mind the fact that Mom and Dad were an "interracial couple." In many ways, my mother had been cut off from the long-term social intricacies involved in the heirarchical relationships among other Japanese, Japanese Americans and other Asian American groups. Some of it was of her own choosing and some of it was because she was married to my father who was Caucasian. The arrival of my brother's girlfriend brought back memories and forgotten stories about the encounters between my father's mother, an English woman who came of age at the height of the "British empire,"

MARI SUNAIDA is a writer, performer, producer, director, and co-president of Pacific Asian American Women Writers—West. She produced the compact disc portion of *High Performance* magazine's "The Verdict and the Violence," special summer issue and "Seoul to Soul" six weeks before the civil unrest last spring. She is currently at work on her new play "Scenes from an Interracial Marriage."

and my mother, who grew up as a privileged daughter of the "Japanese empire." The drama played out in my own family mirrored some of the tensions and misunderstandings that are played out daily between the Korean and African American communities in Los Angeles, dividing even those who had experienced the same tyranny of assumptions first hand.

On March 14, 1992, I brought together for the first time Korean and African American writers in an evening of poetry and performance entitled "Seoul to Soul." For over two hours the writers shared their words and stories with an audience of close to three hundred people representing the diverse spectrum of the population here in Los Angeles. The audience sat and listened, laughed and wept. They bore witness to the pain and anger of the immigrant and slavery experience, to their shared history of oppression, and to the beauty of the human spirit. As poet Lynn Manning said, "I was buzzed for two days after. There was some real listening going on in that room."

How had "Seoul to Soul" come about? I wasn't Korean, or African American. Why had I chosen to volunteer my time and resources over a period of months, as well as recruiting my husband, several cousins and numerous friends, to help produce this kind of an evening? Very simply, I felt it had to be done. A mountain had to be moved. The years preceding that evening had thrust my consciousness into an activist mode, although I was loathe to admit it. I did not want to see myself as "political," or worse yet, a marginalized radical feminist artist of color making loud noises about oppression and genocide. I saw myself as an actress and a writer of short fiction and plays. I thought if I paid my dues, worked hard at my craft and developed relationships with other artists I respected, my work would speak for itself. My safe assimilationist tendencies were in for a rude awakening with the *Miss Saigon* controversy. I was one of the many placard-carrying, petition-collecting, letter-writing Asian actors who protested the casting of a Caucasian British actor in an Asian role made to justify this choice. I also questioned the necessity of casting a non-American actress in one of the few leading roles available to women of Asian descent. The energy generated by our protests was exploited by a shrewd powerful producer to his advantage. He reaped millions of dollars worth of free publicity, tremendous public sympathy and the full support of the theatre establishment who interpreted our protests as censorship.

The myth of the American theatre is that actors should be able to play any role. An actor's job is to inhabit a character and bring it to life. The hidden rule to that is the opportunity is predisposed to those whose ancestry appears to be European-based. There was a lesson to be learned.

I was definitely offended by seeing the hundred-year-old Madame Butterfly stereotype being romanticized and trotted out in different disguises over and over again. I realized then that colonialism was alive and well on Broadway and that the legacy of racism in the theatre would continue unless I and others like myself chose to do something about it. In order to reframe the Asian American experience in late twentieth century America, I had to initiate and produce my own projects and tell my own story as I understood it.

At around this same time, Nat Jones and I began collaborating on creating a theatrical piece about a relationship between an Asian woman and an African American man set in his neighborhood, which is now known as Koreatown. We took field trips near his apartment, ate in restaurants and grocery-shopped together. My feeling was the looks and suspicion Nat experienced in Koreatown were based on cultural misconceptions. His sense was it had more to do with his skin color. I wasn't sure. After the death of Latasha Harlins we decided to put the project on hold and concentrate on our own individual writing. Suddenly, the canvas of our project seemed pale and small in comparison to the real life events taking place. The responsibility of the questions we had to ask ourselves became overwhelming.

I became acquainted with Chungmi Kim through Pacific Asian American Women Writer's—West several years ago. I was impressed by the way she linked up the psychic ambivalence of her spiritual displacement between America and Korea through her poetry and plays. Her lyrical style shared a similar sensibility with Nat Jones. I was very moved by Arjuna's performance piece "Combat Ready," about his experiences as a military advisor to the Royal Thai army during the Vietnam War which I saw at Highways Asian American Performance Festival. During a conversation with him a few months later, the idea of "Seoul to Soul" began to take shape.

From the inception, "Seoul to Soul" quickly gathered its own momentum. In short order, I raised startup funds and went about finding other Korean and African American artists who would be interested in addressing some of the pressing issues concerning both communities. The title "Seoul to Soul" was chosen for the obvious play on words which my husband John and I discovered while trying to create a graphic image to represent a sense of connection between Koreans and African Americans. The Philosophical Research Society auditorium was secured as the performance space and a date was set. Although it wasn't a church, the atmosphere of the hall was imbued with the feeling of persons coming together in the spirit of sharing and worship. I found the perfect host in second generation Korean American actor/comedian

Steve Park, who was familiar with the African American community through his work with Spike Lee in *Do The Right Thing* and on the T.V. show, *In Living Color*.

Three of the artists created new pieces dealing directly with the tensions between immigrant Koreans and African Americans. In her poem, Houston Blue investigated the causes of the decimation of the Black community and her own feelings of desolation, anger and love. First generation writers Ko Won and Sae Lee overcame the cultural expectations and the tremendous sense of responsibility of being a voice for all Korean Americans. They were artists first and they cared fiercely about telling the truth as they saw it. Sae Lee's "Barahm," which means wind-hope, critically examines the effects of the mass influx of Korean immigrants and the creation of a Koreatown over the course of twenty years, in an area of Los Angeles formerly inhabited by many African American families. Ko Won's imaginative reconstruction of Soon Ja Du's state of mind in his poem "Born Again in Dark Tears," illuminates the spiritual consequences of her action. Lynn Manning, Nat Jones and Wanda Coleman focused their work on life as African Americans in contemporary America. They made their claims, presented the truth and took a stand for enlarging cultural consciousness. "Seoul to Soul" showed the willingness of people to come together and helped to counterbalance the media exploitation of Korean-Black tensions.

From the enthusiastic response of that evening, it was hard to believe that six weeks later many of these same people would be caught in the crossfire of the Los Angeles civil unrest in the aftermath of the Rodney King verdict. In the days following the uprising, many of the artists from "Seoul to Soul" participated in community dialogues all over Los Angeles. One of the projects that came out of these dialogues was a collaborative endeavor between Wanda Coleman and myself for *High Performance* magazine's special issue, "The Verdict and the Violence." One year later, on April 28, 1993, the UCLA Asian American Studies Center co-sponsored "Seoul to Soul II" as part of a week-long commemoration of the L. A. uprising.

Vietnamese Zen master Thich Nhat Hanh speaks to the issues of transforming our suffering in this quote from *Parabola*. "The Buddha said that the ocean of suffering is immense, but when you concentrate on transforming it, you will see the shore and land right away."

Born Again in Dark Tears

KO WON

I

The woman was tottering.
She was scared by her own legs.
The very moment her sight was blurred
suddenly, dizzily,
something black—with a flash—
was caught in her hand.
The hand turned black right away.

The whole world,
indeed the whole wide world
only looked black.
The woman's mind was also
becoming charcoal, pitch-black.
She heard in her heart
coals tumbling.

The woman was tempted
to blacken a black color
with a black color
just to make it
blacker and blacker.
She wanted thereby
herself to burn black, burn black.

KO WON is editor of *The Asian American Literary Realm*. He received an MFA in English from the University of Iowa and a Ph.D. in comparative literature from New York University. Former associate professor of Comparative Literature at Brooklyn College, CUNY, he currently teaches at University of La Verne, California. His publications include nine volumes of Korean poetry and two volumes of Korean essays. His latest book of poetry is *Some Other Time* (Los Angeles: Bombshelter Press, 1990).

II

A woman was taking aim
at a woman's life
filled with grief.
She was at once aiming at every
Korean woman's all sorts of grief.

Exactly aiming at
the way of life called immigration,
the name immigration,
double nationalities of Korea and the U.S.,
the language itself that had been lost
somewhere, nowhere, now that
she spoke neither Korean nor English,
and her own resentment
cursing Heaven for this, for that,
all the many black colors,
she was merely taking aim at them
with herself being in black, black.

A second and another second
passing in a flash,
an instant she was aiming
at a thing that is nothing,
vanity of vanities,
and at an empty air,
the woman was on fire herself.

III

"Eli, Eli,
          lama sabachthani?"
A .38 caliber handgun.
Who played the fool?
To nobody's knowledge, Good
Heavens, in less than a second,
a bullet dashed out.
It dared to shoot through
somebody in front.

Having held a gun, the woman acting
against the ten commandments after all,
against her own prayer,
the hand killed Latasha—
a fifteen-year-old black girl;
the hand, now burning black,
had to tear the woman's heart.

The woman wanted to see her blood.
She only wanted to let a sea
of black blood run on from her.
Eli, Eli, the woman
wanted to fall down herself also
and to shed only black blood
with no end,
with no cross visible.

IV

"Oh, no,
not this, please,
no probation.
It's ridiculous to keep me,
the criminal, alive and to cause
all the Blacks
and Koreans to die."

"I must go; I must go.
A sinner who had chosen to come
to a place she was not supposed to be in
certainly must go with no-one's pardon."

"But what,
what is all this in the world?
What's happening to my life?"

V

It was wrong.
Everything was wrong.
And yet someday, the woman from Seoul
was being born again.

Mrs. "Two" on her way to rebirth
had to stand on a new hill of soul
where two turns to one:
neither a Black nor a Korean,
now one Korean-Black.
A woman to be born again
in the beautiful black color,
a color even prettier
than that of a Korean child
born of a Black father.

A descendant of the black bear,
a woman with black hair, a black skirt,
doomed to be born again
as a Korean-Black,
she is crying, wishing not to be
but to be born again
Her soul cries, praying, in dark tears,
in dark tears.

The Arab Clerk

WANDA COLEMAN

It was 7 a.m. I was in a horrible hurry. There was no milk in the house for the kids. I rushed to a convenience store, found the dairy section, got a half gallon and zoomed to the counter. The clerk was a young Arabian man. He rang up the charge on the register. I went into my wallet and flashed all I had—a twenty dollar bill. It was early and he didn't want to part with any change. I got angry. I told him what he could do with his change and where he could stick what. I took my dignity and stomped out, leaving the milk and my twenty on the counter. Realizing my mistake, I went back and demanded the twenty. He baited me with it. I had to apologize for the nasty things I'd said if I wanted it back. I softened my eyes and apologized. I'm a handsome woman and he went for the okey-doke. He handed me the twenty. I let out a stream of brutal epithets. Shaken, he bucked his eyes and in uncertain English, tried to call me "nigger." I laughed all the way to the next store where I got my milk and got on with it.

WANDA COLEMAN is currently a contributing editor for *The Los Angeles Times Magazine* and was guest editor for *High Performance* magazine's special summer issue "The Verdict and the Violence." She is the Spring 1993 Visiting Writer at Pitzer College in Claremont. Most recent books include *African Sleeping Sickness* and *Hand Dance* (Santa Barbara, California: Black Sparrow Press, 1993).

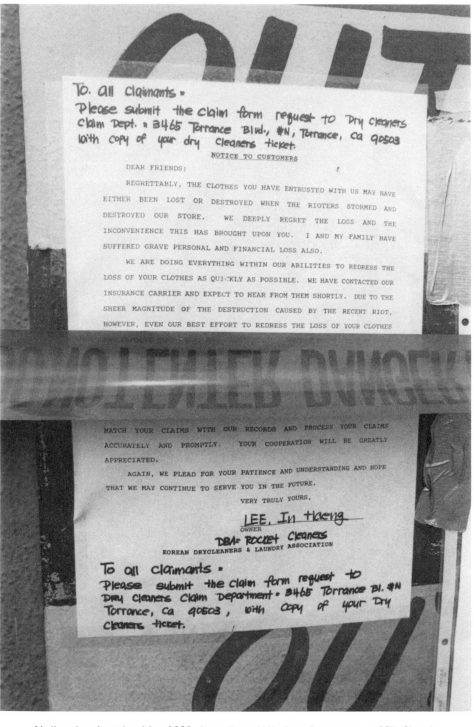

To all Claimants.
Please submit the claim form request to Dry cleaners
Claim Dept. ■ 3465 Torrance Blvd., #N, Torrance, ca 90503
With copy of your dry cleaners ticket.

NOTICE TO CUSTOMERS

DEAR FRIENDS:

REGRETTABLY, THE CLOTHES YOU HAVE ENTRUSTED WITH US MAY HAVE
EITHER BEEN LOST OR DESTROYED WHEN THE RIOTERS STORMED AND
DESTROYED OUR STORE. WE DEEPLY REGRET THE LOSS AND THE
INCONVENIENCE THIS HAS BROUGHT UPON YOU. I AND MY FAMILY HAVE
SUFFERED GRAVE PERSONAL AND FINANCIAL LOSS ALSO.

WE ARE DOING EVERYTHING WITHIN OUR ABILITIES TO REDRESS THE
LOSS OF YOUR CLOTHES AS QUICKLY AS POSSIBLE. WE HAVE CONTACTED OUR
INSURANCE CARRIER AND EXPECT TO HEAR FROM THEM SHORTLY. DUE TO THE
SHEER MAGNITUDE OF THE DESTRUCTION CAUSED BY THE RECENT RIOT,
HOWEVER, EVEN OUR BEST EFFORT TO REDRESS THE LOSS OF YOUR CLOTHES

MATCH YOUR CLAIMS WITH OUR RECORDS AND PROCESS YOUR CLAIMS
ACCURATELY AND PROMPTLY. YOUR COOPERATION WILL BE GREATLY
APPRECIATED.

AGAIN, WE PLEAD FOR YOUR PATIENCE AND UNDERSTANDING AND HOPE
THAT WE MAY CONTINUE TO SERVE YOU IN THE FUTURE.

VERY TRULY YOURS,

LEE, In Haeng
OWNER
DBA= ROCKet Cleaners
KOREAN DRYCLEANERS & LAUNDRY ASSOCIATION

To all claimants ■
Please submit the claim form request to
Dry Cleaners Claim Department ■ 3465 Torrance Bl. #N
Torrance, ca 90503, with copy of your Dry
cleaners ticket.

Notice, Los Angeles, May 1992. Location at Western Avenue near 35th Street
has remained vacant since its destruction. Photograph by Eugene Ahn.

According 2 THE SCRIPT
dreadlocks on Korean's?!
optional.

MELLONEE R. HOUSTON .B.

▲ ▲ ▲

I Hear African Music FOREVER.
Respect To ALL LIFE. We Can Really See with Spirit Eyes.
The TRUTH IS : JAH GOT THE WORLDS .
To *All*, i wish you JAH LOVE.
JAH = THE CREATOR.

▼ ▼ ▼

According 2 THE SCRIPT,
"The Best" is getting "The Best"
Brilliant Colors of. . .clothes from the mall
Parading as Consciousness?!
and All We can Do is—   Accept "the perm"
                              & the Nap's
                              & The Gaps
                              & The Differences
of Who Can't Be with Who—cause—of—What's
and *The Wombs* R Un-Tapped *SACRED* Sources that *Won't*
"*b*" what "*you*" Idealistically Wants
and That which *WE*, Long-For is Long in Dealing with Us.
We "shower—ourselves" Daily
        but 2 NO AVAIL
For Who *KNOWS*, or, Who *SEE'S*?!

MELLONNEE R. HOUSTON aka BLUE: CREATIVIST. Self-deSCRIBEr. MIGHTY-LONG-WAY Traveller. VISIONARYistic From THE HEART via L. A.

Maybe The COSMOS have us—Staked out.

It *don't* surprise me/People*Don't* KNOW They—Own—Story 2 Well.
but people ACT-Like They WANT MO—LIFE—inna—Day.
WE Shall See *What* Becomes of *This ACT*.
ALL us *can write* or re-write Our *Declaration*
as We most Likely Won't "jus—Follow it."
It's cost-effective 2 Keep—Up with "Tom" and his—Jones
since they—like a extention of what We do "4 Love," even.
Read On:
We Bound 2 UnLearn and ReLearn
The "Un-Cola—Thang" that's a smokescreen.
dreadlocks on Korean's
optional

(re: some—"creatures" onna Earth, However;)
Un-Knowin thy-self? Cool—still Resentin *MY BEAUTY*
which gon Any-Way Enlighten Many "against"—they—will
WE can't—help—but—2—SEE *The Decay*, even at disney(ed)
Land cause People 2 Awaken and DANCE.
the—cold—un—enRIPEned, tight-ass—motherfucka's "would provide"
                    "*The Music*"
and NATIONS would FALL (?)
for Lack of Stoppin A FLOW
THE BALL goes ROUND.
                    Come 2 INTERPRET "ME" LOVE
                    "YOU'LL" Have To
                    "U'VE" "No Choice"

still.   dreadlocks on Korean's?!

        "optional"

All Praises Unto JAH. RASTA FAR I. LIVE.

Barahm

Sae Lee

[PROLOGUE]
Barahm,
Barahm,
It is so precious
in your heart.
Barahm,
In between yesterday and tomorrow,
We are standing on a platform.
Barahm,
Barahm,
It allows us to take a breath of
hope,
longing.
Blow
Barahm,
Longing,
Barahm,
Barahm.

Sae Lee, born and raised in Seoul, Korea is author of several books of poems including *A Miner Who Died in a Mineshaft, My Fatherland and the Moon,* with a third, *Seoul 1992,* published last spring. He has served as president of The Korean American Coalition for Culture and Arts and is also an award winning photographer.

[PROFILE 1]
In the mid 1960s,
I lived on Jefferson Boulevard.
While the tragic Vietnam war was going on.
My friends were a handful of Koreans
and an unknown number of African Americans.
We lived peacefully on Jefferson Boulevard
right after the Watts Riot.
Barahm,
Barahm,
Nevertheless, I left the Crenshaw district.
Soon, those streets were filled with unfortunate people
and homicide was almost a daily routine.
I then moved to Olympic Boulevard.
I saw many Koreans who had made
a fortune by their own efforts.
I also saw many Koreans who had brought
a lot of money from Korea.
Real-estate prices were sky rocketing
and houses were destroyed in order to build tall buildings.
All kinds of crime quickly moved in;
Korean merchants were often killed by gunmen,
and the shop owners began arming themselves.
I saw a sad crisis.
That certainly was not the American dream.
Barahm,
Barahm,
reality of dream was unreal.
Barahm,
Barahm,
Time may heal the wounds,
but we have wasted precious time.
The government ignored a horrible war
within the state,
instead the Pentagon kept dropping bombs
on foreign countries.
While I was trying to hear Abraham Lincoln
and Dr. Martin Luther King's voices at the same time;
the majority of people were reading
the autobiographies of Paul Getty and Rockerfeller.
Barahm,
Barahm,

I could not live in the Koreatown.
so many Koreans had illusions;
illusions of money, money,
I did not want to be associated with money-minded Koreans,
Nor loitering young African Americans.
I left Koreatown,
I simply left them.
Most Koreans directly or indirectly
try to build Seoul in America.
This dream is wrong.
The dream must have rationale.
Hundreds of Korean churches selling dreams without rationale.
What is the difference between religion and superstition
Without rationale?
Barahm,
Barahm,
Open your eyes.
We do not want to see another Soon Ja Du.
Let us live up to the true American dream.
The dream must be discovered,
Not made up.
We do not want to see another Rodney King.
Let us live up to the rationale
rather than anguish.

[PROFILE 2]
Didn't we all say that
We do not want to see another Rodney King?
Barahm,
Barahm,
April 29, 1992.
Once T.S. Elliot declared that
Ash Wednesday;
We saw Reginald Denny on an Ash Wednesday.
We saw thousand blazes in Los Angeles.
We saw Korean immigrant merchants
crying in the streets.
Barahm,
Barahm,
What else did we witness?
Manipulator Ira Reiner.
Laughing Daryl Gates.

Half drunken Tom Bradley,
Of course we saw looters,
Animal like human.
Barahm,
Barahm,
How could we human beings be like human?
When can we end the so called "Racial issue"?
Certainly, so many Korean merchants caught in the middle,
Middle of the Black and White issue.
Most merchants were helpless like sitting ducks.
I knew, you knew,
time would come;
but no place to go,
just like sitting ducks.
Barahm,
Barahm,
Reality of dream was unreal.
Didn't we all say that
We do not want to see another Rodney King?
but, We saw another brutal beating of
Reginald Denny on an ash wednesday.

[EPILOGUE]
Barahm,
Barahm,
Between you and I,
Black, White, Brown, Yellow,
Whatever you and I may be,
without separation of ourselves,
We must understand the eternal cry;
"I have a dream!"
Barahm,
Barahm,
Man must live worthy of man.
Barahm,
Barahm,
In your heart
deeply
blow
Barahm,
Barahm,
A genuine dream,

Longing for the future.
Between you and I,
Black, White, Brown, Yellow,
Whatever you and I may be;
We must hold together.
blow
Barahm,
Hope,
Longing,
blow,
Barahm,
It is cycling between us,
In your heart
In my heart.
We are standing on a platform,
Barahm
Barahm.

*Barahm is the phonetic representation of a Korean word which has the dual meaning of Wind and Longing.

Gas station, Los Angeles, May 1992. Location at Western Avenue and 35th Street has remained vacant since its destruction. Photograph by Eugene Ahn.

The Word

Nat Jones

I am parked in the shallows on Ivar and Hollywood Boulevard, I am twenty-five now. I am waiting for the headaches. And the night air feels like razors. I am entering the Baths. I am not ashamed. I am big headed. It is the repetition. I will pay them and they will give me a towel and key. And the rent will be late again this month. I am not ashamed. I will have what you wanted. I am walking up the steps. It has been a day when the past felt too accessible. It felt like a tide in me with the butts and cans and turds that are my memories riding in. I will be what you kept hidden. And the sex will speak to us. I am not ashamed. I am waiting for the headaches. And no one will ever touch us. No one will ever come between us down there.

They dropped him in earth that was the color and texture of the Egyptian #3 he patted on his face every morning with a soured sponge. It sprinkled down like the extra he shook off into the muddied sink. It caked on the coffin with the morning dew. It sank into crevices like his smile lines at the end of the day. They were amazed at how well I'd taken it, my projectile laughter stunned them to a rock at their heels. "Take care of your mother." The tombstones were like so many teeth in the grass's grimace. I popped my gum, giddily wiped what felt like hail from my face, and yodeled unintentionally with my fifteen-year-old voice. There were no words. The words were down there in monosyllables threatening to burn me up, while mother trembled triumphant in her hysteria. And peeked out at me from behind her lace handkerchief.

When she told me, I stood in her pink bathroom, hiding. It was the upward curve at the right side of her mouth, her strut from bedroom to kitchen and back; adjusting the white slip, flicking the light switch,

NAT JONES is a poet and fiction writer and also a jazz singer, actor and dancer. He has performed extensively in L.A. most recently at The L.A. Poetry Festival, Barnsdall Gallery Theatre and Inner City Cultural Center. His fiction has been published in *The Spring Street Anthology* and *High Performance* magazine.

fastening plastic clips on orange sponge curlers, fingernails scraping the walls. I felt the air of an impending trip, the need to rise early, the need to search for dramamine.

"Your father has lung cancer," she said. No reply. "Your father has lung cancer and it has spread to his brain." No reply. "Did you hear me?" Then the light pop of her nylons against the carpet.

I yanked down my drawers, turned on the wall heater, and sat on the toilet seat, because it was close to a fetal position as I could get: because the infantile tilt of my brown upper body into the hot pink wall achieved a kind of irreducibility.

The afternoon of my father's first headache, she poured water into a red plastic tumbler. High on her heels, in her flowered apron, she breezed into their dark bedroom; one hand flat on the bottom, the other wrapped around the cerated edges of the tumbler.

"What am I supposed to do?" she would shriek on our Sunday morning church outings. "You reek of bourbon. What do you bathe in it? You reek. What am I supposed to do?"

She genuflected, placing the tumbler on their mahogany night table; then sidled out with their repressed brimming of ice packs, and aspirin, and phone calls to the doctor. Perched on the side of a bed suffocated with pillows in pink and green cases, I paid him my obedient visit. The lower portion of his face was engaged in some kind of an undertow: the jawbones, the cheeks, the mouth with its discolored crooked teeth, all sucked up to a swell at his forehead and the spray of sleep beneath his half closed lids. I passed him the tumbler. He angled his head to drink. He coughed, then hiccoughed, the tumbler wobbling in his hands. I took it from him and replaced it on the night table. It was a few hours, the tumbler remaining through my dinner in the dining room with mother and the nightly news, before my stiff legged goodnight to him and my accidental sip form it.

So that as I swayed on the toilet seat, I saw glossy photographs from my biology book of amoeba splitting riotously in drops of water. My father's drool became a catalyst for an obscenity of cell reproduction. The tumbler developed a head, brown and thick with paramecium. I had taken the sip, I rationalized, because I was suddenly thirsty, because I had used that tumbler often, because I had assumed it was bourbon and wanted to understand the words it spoke to him. But the truth seeped in, and the tumbler became our dram of poison: the absurd manifestation of a love I had thought only dutiful; acted out in matching stockingcaps at bedtime; the sweet peach-scented pomade slapped flat handed onto our kink, then brushed hard so that the hairs surrendered into waves; the old stockings of mother's cut and squeezed, end tied onto our hands, then tightened with a green penny twisted at the nape of our necks; the runs, ladders of rebellious hairs bristling to the top knot; the chapstick traced thinningly onto our lips; the grudging attendance at his high school alma mater; the nibble at his dirty man breakfast of sausage and blackened eggs, when mother had cramps. I was taller than he, more gifted. He suffered from the eroding effects of his relentless early marriage, his bourbon, his chase for celebrity. His voice became a wide vibrated croak. And his patent leather head bobbed behind a piano, near the darkened wings of a nightclub stage, in a miasma of downbeats and cigarette smoke. I knew that I was meant for more. And to get it, I had to out run a vague sense of doom. The vague feeling that he wanted me guttered. It was only in the midst of his dying that this underground spring, this father and son, welled up torrential and swallowed me in its brackish water and daddy spit. It was only after my sip that I came to believe he had won. I waited for the headaches.

I am not ashamed. I am something out of Hieronymus Bosch. They are buzzing me in. I am big headed. I will be what you kept hidden. No one will come between us down there. No one will ever touch us. I am not ashamed.

I was in our high school hallway at lunchtime, after a quick hit of nicotine in the boy's room: silver with the midst of Colombian, and the tinkle of metal pipe bowls on tile. I was slightly numb at the extremities. I was meeting my Jewish girlfriends. I was grateful for our adolescent morbidity like a thin sheet of black ice; grateful that my father's illness was simply one of many atrocities in our Salinger like dream of gun powdered temples and slashed wrists; grateful for our chats. And when they asked me about him, I told them no. And the words were down there in elegant Jungian phrases from books I had begun to read because I knew there was something terribly wrong. And when they spoke of their synagogues and their bar mitsvahs, I felt the whirlpool suck of his caked complexion and slicked hair. It was the same feeling of descent I would experience when on the subway, the person next to me spoke in their own language. It was as if someone had cut a tendon and I'd go down momentarily losing my grip on the pole. I would spend afternoons secreted in my room devouring foreign language phrase books. Wrapping them around me like inner tubes to keep my head above it.

I offered up my languages to him on one of my hospital visits: feeling that it might be my last chance to hear him say that I was clever, smart—that he was proud of me. And I was startled almost to muteness by a dry-mouthed need for him to see more, for him to see beyond the phrases, for him to hear me like he heard the clink of of the ice cubes.

"*Doke ni sunde imasu ka*?" I pronounced haltingly. "That means where do you live in Japanese."

"Butchy," slurred the morphine; his head trying to escape its neck on the wet pillow. This "butchy" was his nickname for me. This "butchy" was our watermark. This "butchy" always shifted his eyes to that spot just below mine when he lectured me, glass in hand.

"People treat you the way you act. Why 'butchy'," me sitting at his feet collecting charcoal chips from his filters in the ashtray. This "butchy" always shifted his eyes to the murkiness beneath the water-lillies in mother's Monet hanging on the living room wall; where I felt he saw me stooped at the roots of a tree bent with climbing boys; where I felt he saw our fishing trip of the hooks in my legs and the heavy see-sawed silences at the bottom of our rocking boat; where I felt he saw me toweling off, naked and so very small in comparison to him floating like a brown jellyfish in the soapy bath water between his thighs.

I became comfortable with the tableau; me mothering my sick parent; my own floodlit Pieta with mother in the doorway behind the ropes. I became comfortable with the whiz chuck of the machine; its tube down my father's throat sucking bile from his stomach. I told him to squeeze when it hurt; his hand in mine, the palm as dark as the back.

"Fuh, Fuh," slurred the morphine.

This was the first time I had heard him curse. The closest he'd come at home was "God bless America" at a stubbed toe or tipped glass. I had felt that it was in him though; I had felt that he was saving his ability to be out of control, his passion, for his times away from us; for his conversations with his bottles, for him open windowed boozy speeding screams down the West Side Highway at three a.m., for his women who woke up beautifully on bathroom floors at dawn. I had felt that I was not worth a goddamnit. I told him to squeeze, squeeze.

"Thit Thon, Thit Thon," slurred the morphine. Whiz chuck whiz chuck went the machine.

On the day he died, my uncle Tommy told me in the crowded hospital elevator as the metal doors scissored shut. "You know your father died today," he said. I told him I knew though I didn't and missed the rest of the ride up. I heard my mother's sobbings: "What am I going to do now. What am I going to do now," ringing down the hall. I saw her collapsed against the forest green wall. A nurse gripped her upper arm. She motioned me toward the opened door opposite them. The room was bare. The machine was gone. He was an eel, he was so thin. There were air holes in his neck. His body was in the shape of a c. It was the color of pitch and rainbowed green from radiation. The sheets were dingy and tangled, falling to the floor as if the bed were being stripped. And I could see the concentric circles distorting the fluorescent lights above my head. And I could see the white rain of bubbles. And I could feel the pulse of the reverberation. But I could not hear the splash. I knew I had to cry. I knew I had to match mother or be over-swept by her "I now, I now" filling the hall. I knew I had to find the safety of the tableau. I searched for the loss in the only moment I had with him; in the feelings of my seven-year-old body tightrope walking the cracks in the sidewalk in front of our apartment building; I in spotting him huge on the horizon, in the feeling of my legs, warm lotioned and elastic in the midday heat, in the exhultant release gravity caused by my down hill run, in my arms straight above my head leap into him, in the stubble of his chin tickling my stomach, in the touchable sky, in the air smelling of cut grass and popsicle juice, in his chest rumbling and be barreling out beneath my legs with his "butchy", in the word down there aching and boldfaced and bing cherry red, in my saying it with my mouth wide enough to swallow the sun. I could not cry. I could not hear the splash, only mother's "I now, I now" bouncing like radar.

And daddy, I have never gotten over the feeling that earth has blown apart, that the sidewalk might not support me, that the stars are coming down. I am not ashamed. There is a plywood door and bare light bulb hanging through the missing ceiling. I will have what you wanted. My voice will be clear and strong and straight in the hot light. There is a sodden mattress. I am not ashamed. I am Wagnerian. I will be what you kept hidden. I will be that scaly thing beneath your smooth complexion. I will hold men whose skin feels like paper and whose lips do not protect me from their teeth. I will have what you wanted. And no one will come between us down here. No one will ever touch us. I am big headed. I am something out of Orf. I will be what you kept hidden. I will be all curves and fluidity. I am not ashamed. I am waiting for the headaches. I will be that thorny thing amidst tentative pink fingers. I will have what you wanted. And the plywood door will revolve. And the sex will speak our words over and over again. I am big headed, I am not ashamed. I will have what you wanted. I will be what you kept hidden. I am waiting for the headaches.

Street peddlers, Los Angeles, August 1993. Boy is part of a group that sells pillows, posters, and souvenirs all over the city. Location at Western Avenue and Pico Boulevard. IPhotograph by Eugene Ahn.

Combat Ready

Arjuna

My mission: Provide basic infantry training for Company "C" of the Royal Thai Army. Upon completion of training, immediate deployment to Viet Nam. The year 1967.

Right out of Officer Candidate School, as a Second Lieutenant, I volunteered for the 5th Special Forces Company, stationed in Na Kom Pha Nom, Thailand. I figured, what the hell, Viet Nam, Thailand. . .what's the difference? I remember reading an article in my mother's favorite magazine, the *Readers Digest*, about the Domino Theory, if Viet Nam fell to the communists, then all of Southeast Asia would become red. I was ready to save Thailand from the commies. Little did I know that troops from Nam were taking their R.R. in Thailand. Thailand had some of the most beautiful women in the world. I was in G.I. Heaven. Because of my official status, Military Advisor to the Royal Thai Army, I lived in a civilian bungalow, drove a civilian car and had my own interpreter. Not bad for someone who was drafted in 1965, right at the beginning of massive U.S. troop build up in Viet Nam. I was young, dumb, and full of cum. I figured, if I was gonna die, I might as well have a good time and play out all of my childhood fantasies. I wanted to be a warrior. Who knows, maybe I'd be a war hero.

After basic training, I was sent to the Army Security Agency, for advanced training, then to jump school, O.C.S. and finally assigned to the 5th Special Forces Company in Na Kom Pha Nom, Thailand. I was a model soldier. I wanted my family to be proud of me, especially my father. After all, he was at Pearl Harbor when the Japs bombed the hell out of it. My dad was from Tennessee and so was Sgt. York, the World War I Medal of Honor winner. In the movies, Gary Cooper played Sgt. York and whenever the Sgt. York story came on T.V., my dad would make me watch it.

Arjuna is a performing artist, playwright and vocalist. He most recently performed his one man show "Dancing Song for Dead People in Other Worlds" during the "Fire in the Treasure House" festival at Highways in Santa Monica, California. He teaches overtone singing using Hindu and Taoist techniques.

Oh the glories of the celluloid hero. It's sad to see how each generation prepares it's young for manhood by preparing them for war. . .and the movies play an important part in the preparation. Gary Coop. . .I mean Sgt. York, single handedly captured a whole German Division, and like Sgt. York, I was a Christian and I had to rethink the guiding principal of my moral life. "Thou Shalt Not Kill. . . . "Thou Shalt Not. . . . Why could't I be like the warriors of the Plain Indians, where it was considered much more courageous to touch the enemy with an ornamental ritual stick, than to kill him. To kill an opponent was considered a display of weakness, a lack of courage. What the hell, the Bible is full of war stories. Besides, the enemy worships a false God. But I must admit, being raised a Southern Baptist, I was pissed off when a Catholic cardinal blessed a squadron of phantom jets just before a bombing run over Hanoi. I remember when John Kennedy was running for President, we would pray and pray and pray he wouldn't be elected President because he was Catholic. For years, I hated Catholics.

Anyways, getting back to my mission. My A-team set up a six week training course, and let me tell you the training was basic. Most of the Thai soldiers had never fired their weapons before. Not that they couldn't become good soldiers, it was just going to take time. And little did I know that we were not only training the Thai Army for combat in Viet Nam, but we were developing a military establishment that would someday rule the country.

The first week of training consisted of marching, conditioning, getting them familiar with their weapons and equipment. The second week, marksmanship, communications, hand-to-hand combat. . . . Hand-to-hand combat, what a joke. The ancient warrior met his foe in direct struggle of skill, strength and spirit. If flesh was torn or bones broken, you could feel it. And if you had to kill. . .and if you had to kill, you would forever remember the man's eyes whose skull you had crushed. But the combatants in modern warfare pitch bombs from 20,000 feet, causing untold death and suffering to civilian populations and then return to their base hundreds of miles from the drop zone and eat steaks for dinner. Speaking of steaks, I would spend the weekends with my training team, barbequeing at our off base bungalows. I was the only officer among ten N.C.O's. One thing I learned early on as a second lieutenant, take the advice of the more experienced sargents or they can make life miserable for you. I mean, how could I question the advice of a master sargeant who had close to thirty years of military experience. He was O.S.S., dropped behind German lines in W.W. II. A couple other sargents were airborne over Cuba, ready to drop into the Bay of Pigs, but Kennedy aborted the mission. As part of our Civic Action

Program, every now and then we would parachute into a remote village and the medics would treat the sick and at night using our portable generators, we would show movies and cartoons and drink rice wine. Many nights we'd get drunk and they'd tell war stories and the recurring theme in all their stories was how they got fucked up, got busted and lost their stripes. You weren't part of the old guard unless you had lost your stripes numerous times. We had some crazy times together especially with our Teelocs, our Thai Sweethearts. The women who cooked, cleaned and made love to us.

When I was growing up I never dated Asian women. My mother was Korean and my father English/Irish and since we lived in a predominately white neighborhood, I always thought of myself as being white.

This was reinforced by my father, who wouldn't allow my mother to teach us how to speak Korean. I remember in the fourth grade, my buddies freaked out the first time they saw my mother.

One of them said, "Your mother is a chink." I didn't know what to say. Since I was born in Hawaii, I said, "No. She's Hawaiian."

From that moment on I knew I wasn't white. I think this was also the time I developed my split racial personality. Sometimes I would think I was Asian and other times I thought of myself as white. Whenever I would fuck up like break a window or lie to my mother, my white side made me do it. If I cut school or cheated on my homework my Asian side made me do it. If I got into a fight and got my ass kicked, I'd blame it on my honky side. If I was at a dance and nobody would dance with me it was because I was a chink. . .talk about racial schizoid.

My first love relationship with an Asian woman was in the military. I went from dating only white women to only dating Asian women. Being a G.I. in Thailand, it was difficult to date women unless they worked at the bath houses or on the military base. If you wanted to be with a woman you just payed for it. It's a subversive military tactic, the power of G.I.s to spend money exploiting and dominating a poorer people. Another way of fucking over the culture.

My mother really never cared who I dated, but she would remark every now and then, "I hope you marry an oriental girl." For some reason she felt I would be happier. Maybe she thought of me as only being Asian.

In the sixth week of training we went on bivouc, we were in full combat gear, on patrol. We had gone about 100 meters when BAM! There was an explosion. Everyone ran for cover. Someone yelled, MEDIC. We had a casualty in First Squad. One of the Thai soldiers had straightened the pin on his grenade so he could remove it quickly. The pin snagged on a branch and the grenade exploded blowing a hole in his chest where his heart used to be. . .and he was off to join Bill Buddha in Nirvana. At the end of training cycle I submitted my evaluation report of Company C to my commanding officer. After he read it he called me in his office and said, "What the fuck are you doing rating these troops non-combat ready? Do you know what headquarters is going to say?

"Sir, I would never go into combat with these troops."

"Don't worry about it. . .they ain't gonna be on the front lines."

"But sir, I talked with the Sergeant Major and he agreed."

"I don't give a fuck who you talked to, as far as I'm concerned they're combat ready (and he threw the report at me). Now change the fucking report."

"Yes sir."

What an asshole. I felt like saying. "I'd like to see you in combat with these troops you fat fuck." That was it. My warrior dreams were shattered. There was no virtue or honor in the military. The Army's slogan. "Be all that you can be." Should read, "Be only what we want you to be." Then I began to really get down on myself. Maybe I had been too sensitive, too caring. . . . Then it occurred to me, I was of Asian blood, training Thai soldiers who were Asian, to kill Vietnamese who were Asian. My first impulse was to kick the shit out of my honky side, but if I did, it would have serious repercussions on my Asian side. I had to put things in their proper perspective. Let's face it, the history of civilization is partly the history of war. There have been approximately 15,000 wars in the past 5,000 years. That averages out to be two or three wars a year. After all, Asians have been killing Asians, Japanese killing Koreans, Vietnamese killing Cambodians, Chinese killing Chinese. . .so why should I be so uptight? The real issue was not that my Asian or white side was killing, it was me, the total human being, whatever the fuck I was. That was killing. And as Krishnamurti said, "War is but a spectacular expression of our everyday life." I was not only fighting a war in a foreign land, but fighting in a war zone within myself. The hostile duality had to end. I had to make peace with myself before there could be peace on earth.

There are some occult teaching that say the United States was established so that all races could come together, share the same environment, work and play together, love each other, marry, have children. . .repeat the cycle enough times and we would become one people. Then we could scratch "racism" off our list of bullshit life experiences. Now when people ask me what race are you? I say Human. Oh, by the way, I did rate Company C combat ready, but my honky side made me do it.

Some of Us Are Still Wanderers

Some of us
are still wanderers
never finding a home.

Coming from a far country
we are burdened with dreams
shattered
unfulfilled.

Wanting to be home
still
strangely bound
between the parallel
of East and West

how many times we sink
to the bottom
and rise
for another beginning
hiding our wounds and anger
from those who accuse us
of our foreignness.

CHUNGMI KIM received an MA in Theatre Arts from UCLA and has written and produced for television, including "The Asian Hour," "Koreans in L.A.," "Poets in Profile," and received Emmy nominations for "Korea," a twenty-three-part news series and "Korea: The New Power in the Pacific." She is the author of a book of poems *CHUNGMI—Selected Poems*.

Some of us
drift away from the mainstream
never demanding a connection

not knowing
what will become of us
we are driven by fear
for our future
for our children.

Our children
kill
get killed
in the streets
in the ditches
in violence
in despair

while we are running
races
man-made chaos
grasping for our destiny
on borrowed time.

What will become of us?
All of us!

Defenseless
some of us weep in the night
still

wanting
a home.

"It's good to see the bruhders 'ere, man.
For de black man can't find 'is roots in Babylon.
De white man, dem come from de caves of de cannibals.
We come from de garden of Africa."

Jamaican street vendor

On a Beach in Montego Bay

Lynn Manning

My toes sift the morning-cool sands
Of this private beach resort—
Digging it!
Freed from street shoes and the streets that require them.
Rare
Atrican American tourist toes—
Come to commune with the Jamaican brothers;
Come to soak
In the warm waters of black sovereignty,
Black majority.
Knobby niggah toes
Finding themselves outnumbered by pedicured pink toes—
Delicate digits seeking carmelization;
Come to play footsy with the natives;

Lynn Manning is an actor, world champion and international judo competitor, recipient of a literary grant from the Brody Arts Fund and an individual artist grant from the Los Angeles Cultural Affairs Department. His one act play "Shoot," was recently performed at the Hudson Theatre. He is an associate member of the Mentor Playwright's Group at the Mark Taper Forum. His first solo spoken work CD, "Clarity of Vision," on New Alliance Records will be released this summer.

Come to compare post-colonial itineraries
While sipping cocktails of rum and coconut milk.
Jamaican toes,
Black and calloused,
Ascend the trunk of a nearby palm
To fetch the much needed coconuts.
They hazard the heights and splinters for minimal gratuities.
My own toes cringe,
Recoil from their own complicity,
Wrestle with their anger and humiliation.
I must seek refuge from these suddenly white-hot sands;
I make haste to my air-conditioned hotel room
And attempt to soothe these reddening blisters of shame.

commentary

Photograph by Eugene Ahn.

Black-Korean American Relations:
An Insider's Viewpoint

LARRY AUBRY

Death and Violence: Unfortunate Equalizers

For months, tension and violence grew between African Americans and Korean merchants throughout South Central Los Angeles. The killing of fifteen-year-old Latasha Harlins by a Korean merchant in March of 1991 highlighted the unmistakable distrust and animosity between the two groups. The posture on the part of many in the African American community was outrage and anger with little indication of a willingness to reconcile differences.

In June, the killing of Lee Arthur Mitchell by an immigrant Korean merchant, ruled justifiable by the district attorney, seemed to solidify frustration and negative resolve. The most publicized position within the African American community was the boycott of the liquor store, whose owner shot Mitchell following an alleged robbery attempt.

In addition to these widely-known cases, there were other less publicized killings, including that of an African American robbery suspect by a Korean auto parts store owner and two Korean liquor store employees by an African American robber. There were also reported instances of arson, vandalism and extortion against Korean merchants. All the while, African American residents continued to report incidents of disrespect by Korean merchants. Even with the negotiated settlement of the liquor store boycott in early October 1991, communication between Blacks and Koreans did not appear appreciably better.

During the early morning of October 1991 at a gas station on Century

---

LARRY AUBRY is a staff member of the Los Angeles County Commission on Human Relations and a founder of the Black-Korean Alliance, which dissolved in 1993.

This article was originally written before the Los Angeles civil uprising.

Boulevard and Broadway in South Central Los Angeles, a nine-year-old Korean girl was shot by an African American male robber as she crouched on a cot in a small back room. This horrible act brought immediate expressions of outrage from both the African American and Korean communities.

Danny Bakewell, president of the Brotherhood Crusade, who led the boycott of the Korean liquor store, denounced the shooting and said the black gunman must be brought to justice. "This is very, very serious in our community. . . . It speaks to the fact that we have to take a stern position on this senseless violence. It is intolerable and we in the African American community will not accept it. . . . We don't care who's doing it. We don't care who it's happening to. . . . It's wrong and we cannot allow it to continue in our community."

In proposing that the city offer a $5000 reward for the gunman, Councilman Mark Ridley-Thomas stated, "This reward sends a message that we abhor the violence taking place in our city and must take action to stop it. More important, we must take a strong stand against violence against children." John Mack, president of the Los Angeles Urban League, Councilman Nate Holden and other African American leaders also strongly denounced the shooting and violence or injustice of any kind.

The Korean community's response to the nine-year-old girl's shooting was stronger than in the past. Korean leaders also called for an end to the violence and wondered out loud if their previous reactions to the killings of Koreans had been too weak. They also pointed out that many more Koreans had died at the hands of African Americans than the other way around. There is anger and frustration in both the African American and Korean communities, and comparing body counts serves no constructive purpose.

The so-called Black-Korean problem reflects the pent-up frustration of both communities. And, it is a problem that goes well beyond Blacks and Koreans *per se*; its genesis is the racist history and structure of the country which fosters social economic inequality and leaves it to the victims to fashion solutions.

In the context of South Central Los Angeles, all small merchants have difficulty. "Outside" merchants catch particular hell because of the *prima facie* resentment by local residents who often perceive these merchants as opportunistic and successful at the community's expense. It is especially important the "outside" merchants —in this case, Koreans—be responsive and sensitive to the needs of their customers. It is the right thing to do and makes good business sense as well.

The Latasha Harlins killing and the shooting of the nine-year-old Korean girl both focused public attention on the horrible price of wanton violence. (Similar cries of outrage are warranted over the senseless killing and pain which occurs regularly throughout the Los Angeles area, but especially in South Central Los Angeles.) No community can afford a "norm" in which the loss of human life is reduced to nothing more than a conversation piece for adults and children who are so conditioned to the death and violence of their daily lives.

The focus of Blacks and Koreans must shift from mutual blame to concentration on do-able objectives based upon mutual self-interest. Fortunately, the scene may be changing—slightly, but significantly.

The boycott of the Korean liquor store ended and efforts were undertaken to bring closure to the agreement. Councilman Mark Ridley-Thomas, together with Councilman Michael Woo, convened representatives from the African American and Korean communities to assess the situation. Participants decided to meet again in order to submit specific suggestions and recommendations for improving economic conditions; African American and Korean churches have taken up the challenge anew. Their obvious potential for assisting and improving Black-Korean relations should not be minimized.

Emotion is a powerful motivator. The killing of an African American teenager and wounding of a nine-year-old Korean girl may be the events which galvanize the Black and Korean communities toward new strategies and new behavior. Neither community can tolerate the senseless devaluation of life represented in the shooting of these two young people.

Judicial Aggravation

The sentencing of Korean merchant, Soon Ja Du, caused anger, disbelief and outrage throughout the African American community. People simply could not believe that Mrs. Du received no time in jail for killing fifteen-year-old Latasha Harlins in a dispute over a bottle of orange juice.

Superior Court Judge Joyce A. Karlin disallowed a charge of first-degree murder and the jury convicted Mrs. Du of voluntary manslaughter; more serious second-degree murder and less serious involuntary manslaughter convictions were also possible.

It is tempting, but usually pointless, to "second guess" controversial court decisions. And, the losing side often has the right to appeal. But legal options, notwithstanding, the scope and intensity of adverse reaction in the Soon Ja Du case warrant a closer examination of events surrounding the trial, as well as the implications of Judge Karlin's decision for Latasha Harlins' family and the broader community as well.

Immediately following the shooting of Latasha, the media incorrectly and unjustly described her as a possible runaway and truant. This was not true but helped create a negative impression in the public's mind. The universality of the negative reaction to Soon Ja Du's sentence is based in part on a feeling that justice continues to elude African Americans and that an African American life, even in 1991, is less revered and of less value than that of any other racial or ethnic group.

Rodney King's beating by the Los Angeles Police Department, which occurred some thirteen days earlier, diverted attention from Latasha's killing. African Americans were, to some extent, emotionally preoccupied with the Rodney King matter, and their overall reaction to Latasha's killing was somewhat muted. The Harlins' family sensed this keenly— to the point of feeling alone and almost abandoned.

The objectivity of the judicial system was called into question early in the Soon Ja Du case. Initially heard in Los Angeles, then assigned to Compton, the case was sent back to Los Angeles because a judge (White) in Compton determined that Compton lacked adequate courthouse security to deal with the potential tension between Blacks and Koreans over Latasha's killing. However, the judge also stated that jurors and witnesses might be fearful of having to go into the Compton area, which is, of course, predominantly Black and Latino.

The prosecution did not comment on the judge's remarks, but Compton's City Council did. In no uncertain terms, the Council protested that the judge had unjustly defamed the city and in doing so set back race relations in the area.

This judicial travesty exemplifies institutional racism: the judge's statement was low-key and matter-of-fact, but it reinforced prevailing stereotypes about the propensity of Blacks and Latinos to engage in indiscriminate violent crime. (Similar stereotypical elements seem to have been at work in the sentencing of Mrs. Du.)

During the trial, members of the Harlins family were sometimes denied entry into the courtroom. At times, they were treated like mere observers and not accorded the dignity and consideration due a family under the circumstances. One or more members of the immediate family might leave the courtroom during a recess, only to be refused entry upon their return because their seats had been given to others.

This, too, is a subtle manifestation of racism. It may not have been intentional, but the impact was no less real and no less hurtful and degrading to the Harlins family.

Judge Karlin, prior to sentencing Soon Ja Du, talked about the need for "healing" and appealed for peace between Blacks and Koreans. Ironically, the sentence she handed down had the opposite effect. The healing process was made immeasurably more difficult by Judge Karlin's insensitive and shortsighted ruling. Black-Korean relations are tenuous, at best, and the immediate effect of the sentencing was to inflame feelings, thereby increasing the possibility of Koreans becoming the targets of widespread anger.

Judges are charged with weighing all the facts and rendering a just decision. In the Soon Ja Du case, the probation officer recommended the maximum sentence, sixteen years, in part because Mrs. Du displayed no remorse for her behavior. Judge Karlin believed otherwise. She stated that the issue of sentencing boiled down to two questions. "...Did Mrs. Du act inappropriately? Absolutely. But was that action understandable? I think it was."

Mrs. Du not only acted inappropriately, but criminally. She took a teenager's life and was convicted by the jury of voluntary manslaughter. For a judge to characterize her behavior as merely "inappropriate" is highly unique, and indeed, almost beyond belief.

The widespread anger, frustration and outrage in the black community has been directed toward Judge Karlin and not Korean merchants. Credit for this must go to African American leaders who have called meetings and press conferences, and issued statements counseling the community to channel its outrage into constructive activities.

Judge Karlin had the audacity to lecture Blacks and Koreans on their responsibility to one another. She stated, "Latasha Harlins' death should be remembered as a catalyst that must force members of the African American and Korean communities to confront an intolerable situation by creating constructive solutions so that a similar tragedy can never be repeated again."

It is Judge Karlin's decision which will be remembered as the catalyst that enraged African Americans, forcing them to address the perceived racist implications in her sentencing of Soon Ja Du.

Learning from the Death of a Teenager

The broader context within which Latasha's death occurred should be kept uppermost in everyone's mind. South Central Los Angeles is an economic graveyard, ravaged by time and neglect. Government services are inadequate, public education is a failure, and housing and employment are worse than in 1965, at the time of the Watts riots. Drastic demographic changes compound and aggravate the area's problems; new Latino arrivals further diminish scarce resources. In addition, African Americans fear a shift in political power.

This scenario is increasingly common in core urban areas throughout the U.S. Not surprisingly, in this depressed and oppressive environment, crime and violence are disproportionately high. Conditions seem to stun the mind, affecting people's sensitivity to physical and psychological violence. African American youth, especially, appear increasingly unconcerned or unaware of the implications of violent behavior.

However, South Central residents are also extremely concerned about crime and violence, and agonize over the fact that both are escalating. They have come to accept these things as an unwelcome, unfair aspect of their lives.

Even though South Central's citizens are disproportionately assaulted, robbed and murdered, there is rarely a significant or prolonged outcry from the community. Gang behavior is feared but tolerated. And while the needless loss of human life is always tragic, conditions in South Central cause tempers to flare quickly. Pervasive fear, hopelessness and rage too often result in the loss of lives with little provocation.

These killings created a volatile, emotional overlay, which made sober thinking and reasoning all the more difficult. Some people were "thinking" with their emotions, and, in so doing, minimized and even disregarded known facts. Their feelings are genuine and the emotions understandable. However, they make for a dangerous situation, which can cause needless aggravation of race relations in South Central Los Angeles.

A major factor in all of this is the African American community's historical distrust of the police, which was reinforced by the flagrant police brutality against Rodney King. Another factor is the already uneasy coexistence of Korean merchants and African American residents in South Central Los Angeles. Very little is done systematically to improve communication and dialogue between the groups; both Korean merchants and local residents are left largely to their own devices to resolve mutual problems. Efforts of individuals and groups, such as the Black-Korean Alliance, are necessary and commendable, but woefully inadequate. Thus far, such attempts to deal with Black-Korean problems have not generated the broad-based support and/or political clout necessary to make a difference.

Another problem is the media, which regularly skews and sensationalizes stories about Blacks and Koreans who are easy targets and apparently make "good copy." The fact is, violent crime between Blacks and Koreans constitutes an extremely small percentage of total crime in the inner-city. Obviously, the media helps to form and/or influence attitudes and opinions. It follows that balanced, responsible reporting is especially important when dealing with a potentially explosive situation such as that in South Central Los Angeles.

Highlighting violence between African and Koreans Americans, as the media often does, with no reference to other areas of conflict and crime in South Central, distorts reality and does a disservice to both communities. Selective reporting clearly exacerbates Black-Korean problems while at the same time diverting attention from other, more serious problems that beset the African American community.

154

A small number of residents, churches and community organizations were so upset over killings of African Americans that they boycotted the liquor store where Lee Arthur Mitchell was killed. Their feelings were understandable, but the soundness and timing of such action must be seriously questioned. It is doubtful that the community's best interest was served by aggravating an already charged situation without sufficient regard for the consequences to the community itself.

And, there are civil rights implications. Should any store be closed without documented evidence of law violation or other significant wrong doing? Overall conditions in the area, including the long-standing problems between Korean merchants and African Americans, make the former easy targets. African Americans must guard against what appears to be a growing callousness for the civil rights of other people of color, including Korean merchants.

The present climate in South Central Los Angeles lends itself to precipitous, unthinking behavior. Residents are tired of being put upon by continuing social and economic inequities, and many are increasingly receptive to lashing out at the most visible and convenient targets. In this atmosphere, it is all too easy for Korean merchants to become scapegoats for the many ills facing the African American community.

Merchants, including African Americans who are disrespectful, or otherwise abusive, should be dealt with accordingly. Such behavior cannot be tolerated. But residents should not blindly target all of their pent-up frustration and anger against "Koreans." It would be tragic if African Americans, a people with such a long and continuing history of oppression, were to become "Korean bashers," with little or no regard for these people's civil or human rights.

Those with long-time grievances against Korean merchants have a responsibility to separate those concerns from recent killings. Indiscriminate coupling of unrelated existing problems to the community's emotional response to the recent killings is dangerous.

In the absence of a well-conceived overall plan for addressing Black-Korean problems, emotion-driven action will predictably result in further inflaming the community. Except for immediate ventilation by relatively few people, nothing constructive will result from such behavior.

A more effective approach would be to clearly identify the major problems, then develop plans and strategies to achieve sought-after objectives. This requires a unified, concerted effort involving community organizations, churches and elected officials, each assuming responsibility for specific aspects of the plan.

The economic infrastructure, poor education, and housing and unemployment all contribute heavily to crime and substandard conditions in South Central Los Angeles. These areas, too, should be targeted for protest and constructive action, along with the perceived problem of Koreans "taking over" businesses in the area. There would be no "take-over" if African Americans reinvested time, money and people resources in the South Central community. A broader, more inclusive attack on the major problems should be launched as a matter of survival for all the peoples who must live together in Los Angeles.

Rebuilding
Los Angeles
"One Year Later or
Why I Did Not Join RLA"

ANGELA E. OH

I was asked to write about why I never joined the group known as
"RLA." In thinking about the reasons, I wrote the following. I offer
these thoughts with hope and faith in the extraordinary strength of the
human spirit:

Almost a year ago, those of us who call Los Angeles "home" were
stunned as we watched the city burn. In the wake of the destruction,
more than fifty-three lives were lost; thousands of small businesses
were destroyed and estimates of property damage alone exceeded $750
million. The loss of the young life of Edward Lee, a nineteen-year-old
Korean American killed by friendly gun fire, was among the most
poignant symbols of sacrifice made during the riots.

Since April 1992 Los Angeles has been engaged in the process of
rebuilding, revitalizing, healing and recovering from the devastation.
Our progress has been frustrating, painful and difficult to measure. As
a community, we are confronted with some very basic questions that
need to be answered before we can move ahead.

What is the vision for a Los Angeles that works? Where are we
headed? Is there time to craft meaningful solutions and to take care of
the myriad needs that leaped into focus in 1992? Do we really want to
get along?

A number of vehicles for recovery was offered to Los Angeles during
the weeks that followed the eruption in the City. Among them was an
entity first known as "Rebuild L. A.," led by ex-baseball commissioner
and Olympics organizer, Peter Ueberroth. He was appointed by both
Mayor Tom Bradley and Governor Pete Wilson to bring to bear his skill

ANGELA E. OH is a local community activist and partner at the law firm of Beck,
DeCorso, Werskman, Barrera and Oh.

as a master planner. The organization, now known as "RLA," has become the main channel through which corporate America (also known as "the private sector") has funneled its resources in the recovery efforts.

Is there an RLA vision? Yes. It is one that is driven by a corporate model that seeks to provide jobs. By its own estimates, some 50,000 to 95,000 jobs will need to be created to stabilize the economic base in the most heavily affected areas. Unfortunately, almost a year later, less than five thousand jobs have been created. Even worse, each week Los Angeles is informed that yet another company will be closing its doors, moving its operations to a new location outside the city.

Does RLA know where it is headed? The answer is unclear. As one who has been watching its development, the only thing that seems to be clear is that RLA has the ability to communicate with large corporate entities in a way that our local politicians cannot. But this has not translated into jobs or long-term corporate commitments to Los Angeles. The obstacles to secure those commitments are obvious: the rage that continues to seethe in the community; the uncertain political future of Los Angeles and the lack of vision in crafting an economic recovery strategy for the city.

For the public to rely on RLA is a mistake. It is equipped to deal with only one part of the recovery effort. Certainly, it is a piece of the picture that is critical to our success but, it cannot (and should not) be seen as the panacea for Los Angeles.

My decision to focus my energy elsewhere was based on the fact that I recognize my skills and interests are not in conformity with a corporate approach to the challenge facing Los Angeles. Consequently, I have chosen to work as an advocate within my profession and communities from which I come—Asian American (for now, more specifically Korean American), woman and lawyer. These are the places where I believe I can be most effective and where I find I can be sustained through those periods of disappointment and frustration that come with the work of seeking social change.

In the wake of the '92 riot, a myriad of new needs was created: short-term disaster relief assistance; long-term policy and regulatory change in the areas of planning, zoning and finance; social services for limited English-speaking communities and the demand for litigation to address fundamental legal issues in both the civil and criminal arenas.

To further complicate the situation, the tensions surrounding the federal criminal trial of the four police officers accused of beating Rodney King has gripped the city. Is there time to craft a response in the midst of the media frenzy surrounding the possibility of a second riot? The time must be found and it is critical to note that achievements and great strides are being made even though you may never read or hear about them in the news.

As stories about police riot training, skyrocketing gun purchases, the formation of unofficial "patrol units" and rumors of organized targeting for violence abound, the work of rebuilding is continuing. Because of the near-panic that has been created, that work has necessarily had to expand to address the anxiety and fear that has caused even the most dedicated individuals to doubt the worthiness of their efforts.

Unfortunately for us, the stories about accomplishments and change have not made it to the headlines. Stories such as the one of Buwon Kim whose father was brutally beaten in February 1993 have barely been reported. The young Mr. Kim quit his graduate architecture program while his brother, Hyowon Kim, left his theology studies to return to South Central Los Angeles to work the store and to support their mother. Their commitment to protect the local community from the violence that took their father's life is as great as their commitment to bring their father's murderer to justice. The story behind the absence of bitterness and vengeance is extraordinary enough for any publication or T.V. station to cover and gain wide attention. Yet, the story was told only after pushing local news stations.

The building of "Casa Loma" in Pico Union and the fact that three other similar projects to house single-parent families that are poor, hardworking and invisible has gone unnoticed. Yet these efforts represent multi-million dollar investments right here in Los Angeles. They represent jobs, cultural diversity and hope for the future. The story of the creativity behind these endeavors is fascinating to hear. Yet no one has covered this news.

The establishment of a community-based credit union in South Central Los Angeles—an initiative started by the first African American environmental organization in the country—has barely been noticed. Yet this is a significant step in the direction toward creating self-sustaining institutions within the communities that have been neglected by main-stream financial corporations. The story of the persistence, dedication and vision behind this accomplishment would inspire us all.

Where are the stories about the Women's Coalition to Rebuild Los Angeles which will be holding a series of public hearings to give women a chance to state how their agenda can be implemented by the political leadership? This is precisely the kind of bottom-up approach that everyone was talking about a year ago when the cry was, "No more business as usual!" Where is the coverage on how this new approach gives voice to the voiceless and brings women into the planning process and public dialogue in a creative, new way? We have yet to see this activity reported by the media.

Do we really want to get along? Of course we do. The question is how to get there. Each community has embarked on meeting the most pressing need of its members. The resources are not growing, they are shrinking. Given the widespread trauma of the April 1992 riot, burdens have become greater rather than less. Despite all of this, we know that most people do not want to see more violence and destruction. We also know that Los Angeles will likely remain "home" to many. Those among us who see a future in Los Angeles will continue to find creative ways to communicate, educate and advocate.

Sa-I-Gu

SHARON PARK

Sa-I-Gu (APRIL 29): Produced by Christine Choy, Elaine Kim, and Dai Sil Kim Gibson. Written and directed by Dai Sil Kim-Gibson. Co-directed by Christine Choy. 39 minutes, color video (1993).

Sa-I-Gu aims not at exploring the social, economic, and political intricacies of the Los Angeles Riots but rather at simply giving voice to the Korean women who were victimized by the civil unrest. The film recounts the personal stories of three Korean women whose lives were dramatically altered by the L. A. crisis. All three left Korea with big dreams for a better future for themselves and their children but America was not what they had imagined it to be. Their years of toil and struggle to build a better life crumbled on April 29th as two lost their stores and one lost her only son.

The film provides a candid perspective of the experiences and attitudes of Korean women caught in the three days of looting and burning. The victims were allowed to speak for themselves, without bearing the burden of politically correct narrative or sophisticated interpretations of why the crisis occurred. They openly spoke of what they saw and perceived. According to one woman who witnessed her store being looted on the first night, "At first it was all 100 percent Black. After two hours, the Mexicans came. They joined forces and looted all night." The strength of the movie lies in its courage to allow the victims to be honest and frank in their comments, regardless of whether or not it may make the Korean victims appear "racist." Mrs. Hwang, whose market was destroyed during the crisis, expressed her attitude toward Blacks, "I tried really hard to feel love for them but when I saw the way that they acted, I felt intense hatred for them. . .I am mostly mad at Blacks because we were hit by Blacks."

Perhaps the most intriguing issue to emerge from this film is understanding and reevaluating the nature of coalition building among people of color. Many of my classmates have accused this film of being unprogressive,

SHARON PARK is a graduate student in UCLA's Asian American Studies Center M. A. program.

inflammatory, and damaging to the struggle for increased understanding and coalition building among racial minorities. On the contrary, I felt that the film presents a challenge for us to rethink the traditional paradigm of our society as one in which there are essentially two opposing parties— whites against all people of color. The attitudes of Korean merchants as presented in this video points to the reality that, at the present, minority groups do not sense or exist in strong alliance with one another. Among progressive minorities there exists an unstated code of conduct in which it is forbidden to offend or challenge a "brother" or "sister" of color. In an effort to preserve this facade of unity among minorities, the voices of Korean victims are silenced. However, this film allows the victims to speak for themselves and in doing so they expressed deep resentment and a sense of betrayal by both the African Americans and the American government institutions.

The film also powerfully documents the acts of resistance that Korean women victims engaged in during the aftermath of the Crisis. The women were depicted not as passive victims but rather as assertive fighters willing to unite and demonstrate for their rights.

On the other hand, what disturbed me most was the manner in which the film defined the losses that Korean victims incurred. In the first scene, the narrator states that Koreans suffered half of the total financial losses during the crisis. The nature of the losses that Korean women faced goes beyond just material. However, the film focuses heavily on the financial losses and thus contributes to the stereotype of Koreans as greedy and materialistic. In the aftermath of the crisis, the victims have experienced various non-financial hardships in piecing their lives back together again. Among them, they have reportedly undergone tremendous stress in family relations, increased instances of domestic violence, and post-traumatic syndrome. None of these issues were brought up in the film. Material losses were chiefly emphasized and in doing so the film reinforces the mainstream media's portrayal of Koreans as money-hungry people who would kill for a $1.25 bottle of orange juice.

The inclusion of the testimony of Mr. Lee, the family market owner, did the most damage to the film. If the film is about the experiences and attitudes of Korean women, why was this man's views included? He expressed deep resentment against America because he is poor whereas all of his friends in Korea are "millionaires." Repeatedly, he stated that he desires money, "I want to live with money but I have none." His attitude reinforces many of the negative stereotypes of Koreans as materialistic.

The film does not represent a wide spectrum of experiences because the majority of the women who were interviewed in the film are merchants. The Crisis also affected a large number of less-privileged Korean working class individuals whose experiences would have provided a more balanced and diverse view of Korean victims. The women claimed that they had lost all of their money but the viewers do not get a sense of how it impacted it their lives in everyday, tangible ways. For instance, the Hwang family was able to start up a new business almost immediately in the affluent Pacific Palisades district but their experience is far from representative of the majority of Korean victims. In reality, the larger percentage of Korean victims were unable to reopen their businesses after a year.

This Shame
Called Joy

AMY UYEMATSU

—for Thylias Moss

Hand squeezed,
thick with a pulp which clings
to this cup as I tilt it
slowly toward my mouth,
savoring the flesh, sweet
skin against skin—
orange juice.

But I need more assurance
for such small, deliberate joys.
I can't stop seeing
the tape of young Latasha Harlins
being shot in the back over a $1.79
carton of orange juice.
The grocer who kills Latasha
doesn't go to jail and I
can't convince anyone of the crime.
Or of my own outrage.

AMY UYEMATSU aka AMY TACHIKI, editor of *Roots: An Asian American Reader* (Los
Angeles: UCLA Asian American Studies Center, 1971) published her first
book of poetry, *30 Miles from J-Town* (Brownsville, Oregon: Storyline Press,
1992) as the winner of the 1992 Nicholas Roerich Poetry Prize.

My senses grow darker each day.
This lust I cultivate for the ordinary,
the juice of an orange tasting more exquisite
than I ever remember,
cannot be separated from the brutal
death of a child who only wanted
to drink from the same fruit.

I need to acknowledge
my longing and hold joy on my tongue,
this desperate, glorious hunger
to take the whole world in—
even in its meanness—
for whatever it's willing to give.
Let me be grateful for
the tenacity of my desire.

Building Common Ground—
The Liquor Store Controversy

Erich Nakano

When Los Angeles burned for three days of the worst urban rioting in the history of the U.S. in April 1992, it was not only buildings that went up in flames. The fires that blackened large sections of the city also charred the hopes, dreams and livelihoods of thousands of residents. Fragile bonds between communities were not spared damage as well.

One of the most complex and controversial issues to emerge in the aftermath was the rebuilding of liquor stores in South Central. Intensified by sensationalized media coverage, the controversy heightened already tense relations between the African American and Korean American and other Asian communities.

This essay chronicles one community-based effort initiated to address this conflict—the development of a training and assistance program to help burned-out liquor store owners learn and start up a new, non-liquor business.

Understanding the Issues

To fully understand the issues involved, some context is necessary. In a forty square-mile area in South Central, there are seventeen liquor outlets per square mile, compared to only 1.6 outlets per square mile in the rest of L. A. County.[1] This proliferation provides easy access for alcohol abuse. Residents also see these stores as magnets for other negative activities like drug dealing, public drunkenness, sales to minors and other criminal activity. In testimony given in public hearings about some of the stores with the worst practices, residents have talked about drug deals openly taking place in store backrooms, of children purchasing liquor, of violence outside stores involving inebriated customers.

Erich Nakano is chair of Asian Pacific Planning Council Liquor Store Task Force; Project Manager, Little Tokyo Service Center Community Development Corporation; and has an M.A., Graduate School of Architecture and Urban Planning, UCLA.

Liquor stores are heavily concentrated in South Central because of years of government neglect and the vacuum left by the flight of larger supermarkets and other business services most neighborhoods take for granted. This over-concentration of liquor stores has become a lightning rod for the frustrations of South Central L. A. residents in an area with few jobs or meaningful business opportunities. The issue has been a sore spot in the community for at least a decade—long before the unrest of last spring, and before many of the stores were owned by Korean Americans. More recently, the issue has been taken up by the Community Coalition for Substance Abuse Prevention and Treatment. Since last April, the Community Coalition launched a campaign to "Rebuild South Central Without Liquor Stores."

For the Korean American community, the April unrest caused tremendous pain and suffering. Over 2,000 Korean American businesses were damaged throughout the broader L. A. area, representing close to $400 million in damage. An estimated 75 percent of liquor stores that were burned were owned by Korean Americans.[2]

For these liquor and mini-market merchants, these stores represented their livelihoods and often their life savings. They did not buy these stores with the *intent* of bringing harm to the community. Most are recent immigrants, who ended up in these businesses because of economic conditions.

According to a database compiled by the Korean American Inter-Agency Council (KAIAC), two-thirds of these store owners immigrated to the U. S. after 1976, and close to half after 1980. Two-thirds rate their ability to speak English either "not at all" or "somewhat."[3] Like other recent immigrants, many were unable to find satisfactory employment because of a lack of English proficiency and other labor market barriers. Self-employment became one of few viable options to make a living. For many, these stores were their first businesses. These businesses were attractive because they were relatively inexpensive to purchase, and commercial rent in low-income neighborhoods is cheaper compared to stores in more well-to-do areas. Further, a liquor store or small market is easier to operate for merchants with limited English skills.

For these merchants and their families, these stores represented their hopes in the American Dream. In a matter of minutes last April, they went up in smoke.

Trying to Find Common Ground

The Asian Pacific Planning Council, a coalition of human service agencies in the Los Angeles area, initiated a Liquor Store Task Force in an attempt to respond to the controversy. The Task Force was chaired by

Judy Nishimoto-Aguilera of the Little Tokyo Service Center Housing Program and included the Korean Youth and Community Center, Korean Immigrant Workers Advocates, Chinatown Service Center, East West Community Partnership and the Asian Pacific American Legal Center.

Together with the Asian Pacific Americans for a New L. A., APPCON Task Force developed a position paper on the liquor store issue. The position statement was an attempt to understand all the issues involved, and to arrive at a position that could represent *common ground* between Asian, African American and Latino communities based on common principles of justice and fairness. The position 1) supported community control over development, 2) supported the reduction of liquor stores in South Central and compensation and assistance for store owners to relocate or convert to another business, 3) called for an expedited Planning Commission permit and hearing processes to reduce conflict. This position, adopted by APPCON and APANLA, also received the support of the Community Coalition for Substance Abuse Prevention and Treatment, as well as a multiethnic list of other organizations.

But position statements can be meaningless unless they are translated into action. The APPCON Liquor Store Task Force focused on developing a program to facilitate conversion of liquor stores to other businesses. The Task Force worked with merchants, Asian and South Central community organizations, business training specialists, city officials and funders to structure such a program. Finally, on May 28, 1993, the City Council approved funding for the Liquor Store Business Conversion Program from monies provided through the Community Development Department.

The multiethnic program, administered by the Korean Youth and Community Center, would enroll any liquor store owner in over-concentrated areas, with priority to those whose stores were destroyed during last year's civil unrest. It would combine individualized assistance to merchants together with business training and community relations classroom curriculum to help merchants select a new business, investigate it, and go through the many steps to actually launch it. At the conclusion of the program, graduates would be eligible for start-up grants and low-cost financing. The program would also continue to do follow-up with these businesses to insure their success. The program should be able to begin enrolling merchants soon.

Building Inter-Ethnic Relations for a Better L. A.

It is our hope that the program can help a significant proportion, if not most, of the liquor store owners whose stores were destroyed. Through this, we hope to both help riot victims rebuild their lives and enhance their livelihoods, and improve the quality of life in South Central and other communities. Clearly, this program does not solve all the sources of conflict between communities, nor does it wash away the continuing divisions over the liquor store issue. But it is an important step.

Ultimately, the roots of most inter-ethnic conflicts can be traced not simply to cultural misunderstandings, but real issues, often economic conflicts. If we are to improve relations between communities, we must come up with real solutions that address these economic conflicts head on. Such solutions can only come if we can all resist an "us versus them" perspective, and work together to create them. We must strive to find common ground—Asian communities share the same basic aspirations as African American and Latino communities. Where there are conflicts, we must have the courage to apply the principle: we must support for *other* communities what we want for our own community.

In the liquor store issue, what is at stake for South Central is whether a community should have the right to control the rebuilding process and take steps to improve its quality of life. For Korean American merchants, it is their right to a livelihood and to the American Dream of owning a family business that is at stake. We must support *both*. It is important to note that throughout the controversy, Karen Bass and the Community Coalition have made an effort to combat the *racialization* of the issue, and have worked with the APPCON Task Force to find solutions to assist store owners.

In the final analysis, such issues are a test of our compassion. As Asians, we could not help but identify with and feel tremendous anguish at the incredible suffering of Korean American families after April 1992. But we cannot limit our compassion only to our own people. Our compassion must extend to all who face the same suffering and neglect. Only then can the action that we take *strengthen* the common ground between all our communities, and, out of the ashes, create a new and better L. A.

Notes

1. Mary Lee and T. S. Chung, co-chairs. "Mayor Bradley's South Central Community/Merchant Liquor Task Force Final Report" (Los Angeles), November 18, 1992.

2. *Ibid.*

3. Database compiled by Korean American Inter-Agency Council (Los Angeles: KAIAC), 1993.

Black Korea

WALTER K. LEW

*Or your little chop-suey ass will
be a target. . .*

Ice Cube

Last summer, four black cops arrested me because I was "dat chinese
man." You want proof? Get me the money I need for a lawyer—I'll pay
you back extra after I win.

We do win.

▲

EPISODE: After an afternoon of collecting quotations, diagrams, and photos
for an essay on *DICTEE* (the masterpiece by a Korean American murdered
by a security guard in Soho), a night in the Library of Congress's basement
video dungeon, two of the First District's finest holding cages, and
Central Cell Block.

For being "dat chinese man."

IN THE BASEMENT OF THE LIBRARY OF CONGRESS: Sat for two hours while
Mudbrain and crew tried to figure out forms and sign their names. "Do
they want our weight or his?" "I don't know—that's a tough one. I
guess you better go ask the captain." Don't they have to read me Miranda
rights or something? What are one's rights when there's no witness but
four empowered gook-grillers? Twenty more minutes pass.

WALTER K. LEW is a documentary producer, poetry editor of the forthcoming
Greenfield Review Press anthology of Asian American writing, and author of
Excerpts from: Δikth DIKTE for DICTEE (1982), distributed by Small Press
Distribution, Berkeley.

"Do we put in his birthdate or ours?"

"I don't know. That's a tough one."

"I guess I'll go ask the captain. Man, these are tough."

Then it's time for handcuffs and hauling me again for the ride to First District. Young admirer driving the cruiser coos to Mudbrain, "Jeez, I didn't know you had it in you." Badge no. 31 *thirty-one, thirty-one, 7 p.m.* I repeat like a mantra. His name, too—Not mine.

AT FIRST DISTRICT: Crew congratulates itself, "This is good—it sets a precedent." Denied release on citation by Metro PD because "You mean dat chinese man? He hasn't been in the country long enough," despite my documents, sister, and a *Business Week* reporter saying I was born and raised in Baltimore, sixty miles away, despite my Bawl'mer English. "Do we put in his birthplace or our birthplace?" Ain't Chinee, you shitheads, r u F.O.B. from the congo?

No ancestral pine and guardian-graced hillock in Baltimore, 200 ri away, quaked at all this. Sleep, grandfathers grandmothers: I know you sigh already from your own history.

TWO HOURS LATER, STILL AT FIRST DISTRICT: Mudbrain and his fat crew shuffle out of station, smiling, assuring my sister and journalist friend (family name: Hong) that I will be free in minutes. Just working for the public goode, ma'am. *They have a dream! They have a dree-am! That from a gook corpse on the proud flank of Capitol Hill, even morons can one day feast in the glad tidings of proMOtion and like the permed asshole with the citizen's achievement awards covering his left tit who got a hard-on-all-ovah-his-body whenever he pushed me around* ("Stand behind me and put your thUMB out") *even the lowly He and All the Righteous Rest may rejoice as they trample over fallen yellars and ba-baloneyans, always holding high the colors of our world-champion Killah-nation in the cause of of. . .Liberty and Freedom for All. . .No, I mean the NEW WORD ODOR! Hail to the. . .I have SEEN the gLory of the*

Now solely Metro PD's meat, yours Truly, Lew.

Half-nelsoned and shoved away from my sister pleading beyond the door that my rights be honored. Hong notes down names and badge numbers. Dried blood-smears all over the cell's lemon brick.

FOLLOW THE YELLOW BRICK WALL: *DICTEE*, I remember your second image: last wishes carved in the wall of a mine by starving Korean slave children (All for the goode of Japan, ma'am): *Omoni pogoship'o Pae-ga kop'ayo Kohyang-e kagoship'ta* I look down at the steel bench and, after idly glancing along the scattered initials and dates there, discern in the dim fluorescent light that, near the middle, a few *Korean* letters have also been scratched into it. After fifteen minutes of staring and studying, I still cannot make them form a complete word. First syllable: *Mu*, probably meaning "non-," "without-," "not," or maybe it's the *mu* of "soldier, weapon, martial." Then a *ch* and *n*, but there are no vowels in between to make a full syllable. I conjecture that, since one cannot have anything in the cell except the minimum of clothing—even my shoelaces have been confiscated—maybe police came at that point and took the stylus or the prisoner away.

Mu ch n

OFF TO CENTRAL CELL BLOCK: The whole airless paddy wagon to myself, wire tight around the wrists, doubled through my beltloops, marking more flesh each time we bounce through a rut and I'm bumped around the metal plank, window so small and dull I don't know where the hell I am, back-and-forth around the city cuz brainchild forgot my papers.

"You're spending the night here in CCB, no matter what you say." Three hours to frisk, photograph, and fingerprint me for the third time (I think—I've lost track), tortured by "Married with Children" and Arnold S.'s "Commando" on the one-finger-typing officer's tube, though I enjoy the scene where Arnoould's high-heeled sidekick blasts open a paddywagon with an anti-tank bazooka.

Some Latino and Black youngsters I'm being processed with complain about their treatment.

"So sue us, go ahead and sue the whole fuckin department," the sandwich munching officer grins. "Do you know how HIGH the stack of cases waitin to be heard is?"

He lifts his free hand about four feet above the desk. (Me? I just want his fuckin sandwich.)

"Yeah, maybe you'll get heard two or three years from now. And you'd better have a good LAWYER too! We're the federal government!"

Here we go. Just like a Bronson film. Big beautiful belaying pin switches to open and shut cages from a distance, brass showing through where the paint's chipped.

"Officer, put him in here with me, I'm LONEsome."

"Sorry, I don't assign the cells."

Mine is number 22, Jim Palmer's old number! The officer performs his most helpful service of the day: passing single cigarettes back and forth like lacing up a high-top as he walks along between the two rows of cages, twenty-five cents each.

IN CELL 22: To my surprise, I find my brothers of this evening in the many-throated, constantly thrusting and sighing conversation rolling like a wave up and down between the cages. A red bandanna'd gang member ("He's a SCHOLAR!") asks me into their banter, and I quickly conjoin my own solos of sympathetic cluck. They laugh and I laugh: we share our stories of false apprehending.

After a cup of Hi-C (orange color) for dinner, I lay down on a perforated metal frame (my bunk) in water and cigarette ash. For a night of conjuring poems—but for whom? I have no listening *volk*. For the bantering brothers here, then, endlessly joking black boys and brown boys, all sad inside if you listen close enough, but most of all the invisible one with the Korean blade who has drifted along with me from First District's yellow brick, forever laying the dark puzzle out before me like a scarred nameplate or gravestone so broad it blocks off the whole field of vision.

Mu ch__n

Answer this, s/he pleads, I too don know what I'm
spelling out   Please complete for me so I short bars
of light flicker in the cigarette smoke free of this
pain of writing what I don know that etches itself
into bones of my arm my hand

mu ch n

MAYBE SINCE THEN I have passed a brother or sister on the street, that very pattern of scarring weight and need altering a bit the swing of his or her arm on one side, slowing by just the width-of-a-moment the acceleration with which a hand lifts or "warms itself around a cup of coffee."

MU CH N

I guess and gaze, present it to others
Ajoshi, i kos-ul chom pwa chuseyo!
Still have not made up our mind.

(1991)

No Justice

Miriam Ching Yoon Louie

"Student's Killer Freed!"
Screams *New York Times*
Front page headline
Piercing the heart
Tearing an open wound
A gaping aching hole
Releasing yet another
Wave of nausea
Empty rage
Powerlessness
Shame and memory
Of every instant replayed
L.A.P.D. beating Rodney King
Heart of Dixie lynching style
In a circle
Soon Ja Du shooting Latasha Harlins
Because of a lousy bottle of orange juice
In the head
L.A./California/American dreamin' shooting up
In flames
Wish the numbness of repetition
Would deaden the pain
But it doesn't.

MIRIAM CHING LOUIE works at Asian Immigrant Women Advocates which is spearheading Garment Workers Justice Campaign and a boycott against Jessica McClintock, Inc.

Yoshi
I'm so sorry
That the white man
Who blew you away with a .44 magnum
"The biggest handgun made by human beings"
One fatal minute
After your trusting finger
Touched his doorbell
Supposedly to defend
His white wife's white womanhood
He walked away clean
As a rat's ass in Baton Rouge, Louisiana
Freed by an all-white jury.

You wore a white 3-piece suit
A Japanese exchange student
Headed for an American Halloween party
Dressed as John Travolta's
Saturday Night Fever's
Disco dancing fantasy movie character
From Bensonhurst
Where they killed Yusef Hawkins for real
For being the wrong color
In the wrong place
At the wrong time, Yoshi
Just like you.

Just like Darío Miranda Valenzuela
Esposo y papi
For crossing the border at the wrong time
His white Border Patrol killer pumped
Twelve semi-automatic AR-15 bullets
Into his back
Before hiding his body
Again freed
By an almost all white jury in Tucson, Arizona
Save one Mexican-American
Who doesn't realize
It was the border who crossed Darío/México
Coroner's report said his clenched fists
Proved Darío died in agony.

Like Luyen Phan Nguyen
Nineteen-year-old pre-med student
For not liking to be called "Viet Cong" & "Chink"
At a party in Coral Springs, Florida
Fifteen white boys chased/beat/kicked him to death.

Like Nisei Junko Nakashima
José Sangia and Miguel Lomeli
Two Mexican workers at her nursery
For not being "American"
Shot to death by a white man in Watsonville, California
Dressed in camouflage fatigues
Armed to the teeth
He then killed himself.

Like those little Southeast Asian kids
Rathanan Or, Thuy Tran, Sokhin An
Deun Lin and Ran Chun
For being on the school yard
When another crazy white man in fatigues
With an assault rifle made Stockton, California
Another killing field.

Like Robert Buchanan
For being a 17-year-old Thai-Eurasian
Beaten and stabbed to death
By two white skinheads in Olympia, Washington
Although police "can find no racial motive."

Like Thanh Nguyen
For looking like a "gook" and "faggot"
Strippped and shot
Up against the wall in Dallas, Texas
Execution style.

Like Thong Hy Huynh
For being a kid riding his bike
Wrong place, wrong time in Sacramento, California
Like Jim Loo
For being mistaken for a "Viet Cong" though he was Chinese
By the brother of a white Vietnam vet in North Carolina

Like Vincent Chin
For being mistaken for "you fucking japs are taking away our jobs"
By two white unemployed auto workers in Detroit, Michigan
After years spent working on his case
His grieving mom Lily
Returned to China bitter because
"In America there is no justice"
But the victims are many.

To you, Yoshi
And to your parents, Mr. and Mrs. Hattori
Mournfully I apologize
Sorry, sorry, sorry
Because you came here so trusting
To learn about America.

Sorry because after they shot you
Your killers closed their door
Letting you bleed to death in their carport
Staining your pure white suit
With your crimson red blood.

Sorry because the white jury delivered the verdict
Like the Dred Scot decision over a century ago
That you had no rights
A white man was bound to respect.
Sorry because in this country
There is no gun control
No killer cop control
No border violence control
No racial hatred control.

Sorry because even a simple language mistake
(Your killer said "Freeze!" not "Please!")
Can kill you dead
Like it did you and the brother
Of Gregorio Cortez in Tex-Mex territory.

Sorry because despite the street heat warning
"No Justice, No Peace!"
We are so wretched
So pitiful

So weak
There is only
No justice, no justice, no justice. . .

SOURCES: *New York Times*, May 24, 1993; *Network News* (National Network for Immigrant & Refugee Rights, January-February 1992; and *CAAAV Voice* (Committee Against Anti-Asian Violence), Fall 1992.